D0360247

# THE BEST IS YET TO COME

### Growing Older with Joy and Fulfillment

— LORENE HANLEY DUQUIN —

Copyright © Lorene Duquin
All rights reserved.

Published by The Word Among Us Press
7115 Guilford Drive, Suite 100
Frederick, Maryland 21704

24  23 22 21 20  1 2 3 4 5

ISBN: 978-1-59325-379-0
eISBN: 978-1-59325-380-6

Scripture texts used in this work are taken from The
Catholic Edition of the Revised Standard Version of the
Bible, copyright © 1965, 1966 National Council of the
Churches of Christ in the United States of America. Used by
permission. All rights reserved worldwide.

Design by Suzanne Earl

No part of this publication may be reproduced, stored in
a retrieval system, or transmitted in any form or by any
means—electronic, mechanical, photocopy, recording, or
any other—except for brief quotation in printed reviews,
without the prior permission of the author and publisher.

Made and printed in the United States of America

Library of Congress Control Number: 9781593253790

To my husband, Dick, with gratitude and lots of love.

# TABLE OF CONTENTS

# Introduction

Is the best yet to come? What does it mean to grow older with joy and fulfillment? These are the essential questions that this book explores.

As I began the research, I quickly discovered that aging is a hot-button topic. Some people did not want to think about aging, let alone talk about their experiences of getting older. But the things that they did say revealed that they had accepted some modern myths that depict older people in negative ways. It was pretty obvious that they were trying to distance themselves from those negative stereotypes.

Other people were excited to talk about their experiences of getting older. They saw this time of their lives as a chance to be the person they had always wanted to be and a chance to do the things they had always wanted to do. They talked about the ways older people today are redefining what it means to age and smashing the stereotypes that depict older people as grouchy, feebleminded, and unattractive.

These folks told me they are rewriting the script that dictates what retirement means and when retirement should happen—if ever. They are living healthy, active lives. They are finding meaning and purpose in who they are and what they do. And they are discovering that their faith in God not only sustains them but also inspires them in ways they never dreamed possible.

Interestingly, some of the people who initially didn't want to talk about aging changed their minds when I shared the positive ways other people were approaching this stage of life. They began to recognize some of the positive aspects of their own aging process.

I started to see this book as a kind of travelogue highlighting the wide variety of things people experience on their journey into what many call their "wisdom years."

Throughout this book, I cite current research studies that reveal amazing new information about the aging process. But the real experts in this book are the people I interviewed who shared their own stories, insights, and advice. They talked about their joys and their sorrows, the fears they face, the risks they take, and the decisions they make. They shared intimate details about their faith and their family relationships. Some of them asked that their experiences and advice be used anonymously, and I have honored those requests.

In the end, I pulled together the background research and interviews into a series of short chapters on a wide range of topics that explore the questions, concerns, opportunities, and adventures that people face as they move into the later stages of life.

Some people will read this book from beginning to end. Others will read only the sections that apply to their own circumstances. Either approach is okay. There are also questions for reflection at the end of each chapter for people who want to use the book as part of a discussion group.

No matter how you approach this book, it is my hope and prayer that the Holy Spirit will inspire you in ways that will increase your joy and fulfillment throughout the rest of your life.

**Lorene Hanley Duquin**

# CHAPTER 1

# Stages of Life

Joe Buscaglia has never forgotten the framed picture on the wall in his grandfather's tailor shop. "It showed steps going up on one side and steps going down on the other side," he explains. "On each step was a man at a different age. On the first step the man is an infant, and each step shows him growing up. At the top the man is middle-aged. Down the stairs on the other side, the man gets older. The oldest man at the bottom looks a lot like the infant."

The words on the picture were written in Italian, so Joe never knew what they said, but the image made such an impression on Joe that it formed his outlook on life. "My philosophy is that as you go along in life, you are just at different stages," he says. "At each stage, you do what you need to do in order to live your life. There are good things and bad things about each stage. Whatever step you are on, enjoy the moment. It's just another stage in life."

## Understanding Stages

The idea of life being divided into stages goes back to ancient times. Around 600 BC, the Greek statesman and poet Solon identified ten stages of life. Hippocrates listed seven stages. Aristotle boiled it down to three—youth, the prime of life, and old age.

Throughout the centuries, new theories about the stages of life have evolved. Today social scientists are still not in agreement as to the number of stages, but they agree that there are different physical, social, and behavioral elements in each stage. To illustrate these elements, let's take a closer look at Joe's life.

- From a physical standpoint, Joe has gone through the stages of childhood, adolescence, young adulthood, and middle age, and he is currently in a stage identified as late adulthood.
- From a social perspective, Joe is no longer in an active stage of being a son because his parents have died. But Joe is still a husband, father, grandfather, friend, neighbor, and volunteer.
- On a behavioral level, Joe has passed through stages of being a student and teacher. He is now in retirement, but he is busy with local politics, historical preservation, furniture restoration, travel, family, friends, and yard work.

One of the downsides in Joe's current stage of life is type 2 diabetes, a genetic condition that he inherited from his father. "I take care of my health," Joe explains. "That's what my stage in life says I should be doing right now, so that's what I do. Accepting the state of life you are in sure makes things easier."

Steven McEvoy agrees. He was thirty-three years old when he married. His three children were born when he was in his late thirties and early forties. Many people in his age group are beginning to think about retirement, but Steven still has a family to support. "I think each stage of life has benefits, issues, and concerns," he says. "I am trying to instill an appreciation for that in my children. I am trying to live an example of enjoying the journey. I enjoy it with setbacks, pitfalls, victories, and all. I think the best is learning to be, and to be good at being, no matter what age or stage of life you are in."

People who accept whatever stage they are in often describe themselves as being comfortable in their own skin. They feel grounded and peaceful.

"I believe that I came into my own when I turned fifty," one woman says. "I knew who I was, and I had the wisdom and experience to be of value to those who wanted my insights. My wisdom and experience took me to places I never thought I would go, and I felt I was growing into who I was meant to be."

## Transitions between Stages

When we move from one stage to another, we often feel unsettled. Mary Virginia is an attorney who is moving out of her fifties and into her sixties. "I am at the tail end of raising my family," she says. "The day-to-day responsibilities of work, caring for kids, and home have lessened. I have more time to discover how I would like to spend my time. However, I sometimes feel at loose ends because of this. I was used to the routines of motherhood and child care, and now I don't have that."

Mary Virginia is preparing to move into a new stage when her last child goes to college. She is already looking for meaningful volunteer activities. She sees her next stage in life as a time to deepen her faith, and she is looking forward to "new adventures and new paths."

Joe McBride understands how difficult transitions can be. As a high school administrator and coach, he used to see kids struggling through life transitions when they came back in November to visit after having graduated the previous June. "The kids who came the most and stayed the longest were the ones who were not ready to move into the next stage of their lives," he says. "They wished they were back in high school. They wanted to go back, like Bruce Springsteen, to the 'glory days.'"

Joe describes their struggle as a metaphor for anyone moving into a new stage in life. People need to let go of the past and embrace what the next stage of life offers. "There is a time and a place for everything," he says. "I loved all the jobs I had as an educator, but it was time for it to be over and done with. Now I love doing other things. I am on the grandpa circuit. I live in Maryland. I have a son in Wisconsin and a daughter in North Carolina. I am free to travel to see them whenever I want. I look forward to whatever life brings to me."

## A Sturdy Foundation

Every stage we go through builds up a solid foundation for the current stage. We can't detach ourselves from what was. The past is part of who we are today. But if we keep wishing we were back in the past, we are going to be paralyzed.

"Parts of getting older I hate," one woman admits. "I hate the aches and pains and the bodily functions that don't work the way they used to. I hate the amount of time that has gone by since I saw family members who have died. But I wouldn't go backward. I would not want to relive any part of my life. I appreciate what I have and where I am now."

Ellen Prozeller embraces everything she has experienced in her life—the good as well as the bad. "You realize those things that seemed so important in your younger years don't seem so important now," she says. "Living life, you make mistakes, encounter problems, fail, and succeed. You also learn to separate the big important things in life from those that don't matter at all. You encounter suffering, death, and losses. But these experiences often are rewarded with a level of clarity and wisdom lacking in your younger self."

Beth Mattingly finds a new appreciation for the way her life has unfolded. "We can look back and be grateful that certain things didn't happen the way we hoped they would," she explains. "I can remember praying that this guy I was dating at the time would be the one, and he wasn't, so I was devastated. But looking back now I can see it would have been a disaster!"

Teri Donner agrees. "You don't understand things that happen in your life until you can look back on them from a different stage," she says. "One of the best things about getting older is the ability to learn from the past."

## Something to Ponder

For everything there is a season, and a time for every matter under heaven:

a time to be born, and a time to die;

a time to plant, and a time to pluck up what is planted;

a time to kill, and a time to heal;

a time to break down, and a time to build up;

a time to weep, and a time to laugh;

a time to mourn, and a time to dance;

a time to cast away stones, and a time to gather stones together;

a time to embrace, and a time to refrain from embracing;

a time to seek, and a time to lose;

a time to keep, and a time to cast away;

a time to rend, and a time to sew;

a time to keep silence, and a time to speak;

a time to love, and a time to hate;

a time for war, and a time for peace.

—Ecclesiastes 3:1-8

## Questions for Reflection

1. How would you describe your current stage of life?

2. What are the good things and the bad things about your current stage of life?

3. In what ways have previous stages laid a foundation for where you are today?

# CHAPTER 2

# How Old Is Old?

Ann Blask admits that when she was about to turn fifty, she started to feel "kind of old and depressed." But that glum outlook changed the day Ann, who owned her own travel agency, booked a ski trip to Aspen, Colorado for a client. Ann remembers warning the woman that lift tickets at Aspen were up to $100 a day.

"I don't care if they go up to a thousand dollars," the woman replied. "I'm eighty-five, and skiing at Aspen is free for anyone over eighty!"

Today, Ann is in her seventies, but she thinks of herself as being forty. "I can't believe I am old, and I refuse to dwell on it," she says. "When someone tells me they are old, I tell them I can't say that about myself. I don't want to reinforce the idea that I am old."

## Is Age Just a Number?

The age at which people get "old" depends on who is doing the calculations. In a recent study[1] of over half a million people, ranging in age from ten to eighty-nine, researchers asked,

- the age participants would ideally like to be,
- the age participants feel,

- the age participants hope to live to, and
- how old other people think the participants are.

The results showed that older adults consistently considered themselves to be younger than their current age. They also extended the age at which they believe people move from middle age to old age. For example, children and teenagers might tell you that middle age begins at thirty and old age begins at fifty. Older people insist that middle age ranges from ages forty-six to seventy. They consider the "young old" to be ages seventy-one to eighty-five, and the "old" to be over eighty-five. Older adults also estimated that they would live to an older age than the younger groups estimated.

In a recent survey,[2] Pew Research found that 60 percent of adults over sixty-five said they felt younger than their age, 32 percent said they felt exactly their age, and 3 percent felt older. Nearly half of those over fifty said they felt ten years younger. A third of those ages sixty-five to seventy-four said they felt between ten to nineteen years younger. One out of six said they felt twenty years younger!

## Is Age Just a Category?

How old you are can also depend on how your age is calculated. Health professionals and social scientists have identified several different age classifications.

- Your chronological age is the actual number of years you have lived. If your birth certificate says you are sixty-five, this is your chronological age, and you can't alter that.

- Your biological age is related to your physical condition. It calculates how your body functions in relation to your chronological age. You may be sixty-five years old, but because of your physical condition, chronic illnesses, or lifestyle choices, your biological age might be ten or more years younger or older.

- Your psychological age reflects your ability to learn, to remember, and to deal with your emotions. People who shut themselves off from learning new things or deal with their emotions in a negative way are going to register an older psychological age than people who remain active and positive.

- Your social age reflects society's expectations of what life events should take place at a given time. There might be an expectation that people will retire at sixty-five or sixty-six, but that doesn't mean you have to retire at that age. You can alter your social age by doing the unexpected, such as working until eighty, taking college classes at seventy, or starting a new business at sixty-two.

## Mind over Matter

Satchel Paige, the baseball star, broke into the major leagues at age forty-two and played until he was in his late fifties. In an interview with the *Plain Dealer* in Cleveland, he posed this intriguing question: "How old would you be if you didn't know how old you were?"

Then he answered his own question by saying, "Age is a question of mind over matter. If you don't mind, it doesn't matter."[3]

Eighty-three-year-old Chloe Giampaolo agrees. She admits to having a few health issues, but she focuses on the positive aspects of aging. "I tell younger women that the most interesting things I've done in life, I've done since I turned fifty!" she says.

## Not a Disease

One of the biggest misconceptions about getting older is that aging is a disease. But old age is not a disease any more than childhood, adolescence, or middle age is a disease. You don't die from old age. You die from diseases or conditions that cause a breakdown in your bodily system.

A study at Yale University found that people who thought positively about aging extended their lives by over seven years.[4] On the flip side, a study at Trinity College in Dublin found that negative attitudes about aging affect physical and cognitive health in later years.[5] Study participants with negative attitudes about aging had slower walking speeds and lower mental abilities than participants with positive attitudes.

If there is a lesson in all of this, it is that feeling positive about your age—no matter how old you are—is good for you.

# Something to Ponder

Your true identity is as a child of God. This is the identity you have to accept. Once you have claimed it and settled in it, you can live in a world that gives you much joy as well as pain. You can receive the praise as well as the blame that comes to you as an opportunity for strengthening your basic identity, because the identity that makes you free is anchored beyond all human praise and blame. You belong to God, and it is as a child of God that you are sent into the world.

—Henri J.M. Nouwen[6]

## Questions for Reflection

1. At what point in life do you consider someone to be old?

2. How old do you feel?

3. In what ways does your biological age, psychological age, or social age differ from your chronological age?

# CHAPTER 3

# Sister Says . . .

Sr. Linda LaMagna was fifteen years old when she entered a Carmelite convent in 1962. Over the years, she has received a bachelor's degree in elementary education, and she has taught elementary school for fourteen years. After receiving a master's degree in pastoral ministry, she worked for the next thirty years in seven different parishes. She currently serves as the Diocesan Coordinator for Evangelization and Catholics Returning in Altoona, Pennsylvania. After Sr. Linda retires, she plans to work as a spiritual director.

"I thank God that I have had the opportunity to explore many professions," she says. "As a Carmelite, I have embraced a life of prayer and ministry. I love being active in Church ministry rather than being cloistered. I am a people person, so I enjoy social gatherings. I find that people empower me, lift my spirits, and give me a spiritual energy."

To stay healthy, Sr. Linda joined Planet Fitness. "I am usually there exercising at least three days a week," she says. "I enjoy long walks. I enjoy dining with my good friends. I enjoy my vacation by the ocean each year, and I attend many, many socials. I also meet up with family members every other Saturday evening to go out to eat, and then we meet at my brother's house for dessert, coffee, and family conversation."

When asked what advice she would offer to people entering the final quarter of their lives, she says, "Take on as many challenges as you can. God will provide the wisdom and the grace to achieve them."

Sr. Linda epitomizes what researchers have discovered about aging in a unique long-term and ongoing study of nuns.

## The Nun Study

In 1986, Dr. David Snowdon launched an intensive study of the School Sisters of Notre Dame.[7] He was trying to understand why some sisters retained their mental abilities into old age while other nuns deteriorated. The sisters were ideal study participants because they lived and worked in a similar environment. They were celibate. They didn't smoke or abuse alcohol. The files at the motherhouse contained detailed personal histories, medical records, and records of educational opportunities and work experience for each sister. The nuns also had a strong sense of purpose in their lives and a deep desire to help other people.

Dr. Snowdon originally limited his research to studying the nuns' files, but he quickly realized that the most important information could be obtained only if the nuns agreed to donate their brains for examination after death. When Dr. Snowdon proposed the idea at a meeting with all the sisters, there was dead silence in the room. Then one of the sisters said, "Well, of course he can have my brain. What good is it going to do me when I am six feet under?" Another sister agreed. "He is asking for our help. How can we say no?"

A total of 678 sisters, ranging in age from 75 to 103, volunteered for the study. In addition to donating their brains, they agreed to annual medical examinations including bloodwork and cognitive assessments, as well as to informal periodic interviews.

The preliminary results of the postmortem brain analyses astounded the researchers. The brains of sisters whose cognitive tests were normal when they were alive contained tangles and plaques associated with Alzheimer's disease. The findings led researchers to the conclusion that a nun's physical and mental activity into old age played a role in allowing her brain to continue functioning without dementia, even when physical signs of Alzheimer's disease were present.

## WHAT IS DEMENTIA?

According to the National Institute on Aging, dementia is a decline in mental functioning that affects a person's daily life. Dementia becomes more common as people get older, but dementia is not a normal part of the aging process. Alzheimer's disease is the most prevalent form of dementia. Other types include vascular dementia, which is caused by cardiac problems, circulatory problems, or strokes; Lewy Body dementia, which is often associated with Parkinson's disease; and frontotemporal disorders, which are caused by damage to nerve cells in the brain.

## The Example of Sr. Mary

In a review of his research, Dr. Snowdon recounted the story of Sr. Mary, one of the first sisters who maintained normal cognitive function and good short-term memory while she was alive, but whose brain, when examined after her death, contained significant evidence of Alzheimer's disease.

Sr. Mary retired from teaching at eighty-four, but she continued to be actively involved with the other sisters in her community and with her family members. Sr. Mary liked to tell stories and offer advice. She was lighthearted and had an infectious laugh—even though she suffered from cancer and heart disease. She was an avid reader and stayed current with world events. She believed that an important part of her purpose in life was to pray. She used a map and a globe to pray for people around the world. She was 101 when she died.[8]

## Lessons Learned

The results of the Nun Study suggest that exercise, a healthy diet, avoiding alcohol and tobacco, having a strong purpose in life, maintaining social support with a strong network of friends, and receiving ongoing medical care may be factors in preventing cognitive deterioration in old age.

But Dr. Snowdon admits that he learned something more profound from the sisters. On a personal level, he learned that old age is not something to fear. "It can be a time of promise and renewal, of watching with a knowing eye, of accepting the lessons that life has taught and, if possible, passing them on to the generations that will follow."[9]

## THE RESEARCH GOES ON[10]

Today, the work of the Nun Study continues at Rush University in Chicago with a new study that involves 1,350 participants from a variety of religious orders. In addition, the Rush Memory and Aging Project is currently studying nearly 2,000 lay people from different races and backgrounds. Researchers are looking for clues as to what causes the plaques and tangles of Alzheimer's and what can be done to halt the disease process. They're investigating emotional factors such as stress and depression, physical factors such as chronic illness, lifestyle factors such as diet and activity levels, and genetic factors.

In a study presented in July 2019 at the Alzheimer's Association International Conference in Los Angeles, the Rush University researchers reported that people who exercise, adopt a healthy diet, refrain from smoking and alcohol, and engage in stimulating mental activities decreased their chance of developing Alzheimer's disease by 60 percent.

## Something to Ponder

Do not think about what will happen tomorrow, for the same eternal Father who takes care of you today will look out for you tomorrow and always. Either he will keep you from evil or he will give you invincible courage to endure it. Remain in peace; rid your imagination of whatever troubles you.

—St. Francis de Sales[11]

## Questions for Reflection

1. In what ways does Sr. Linda LaMagna's lifestyle reflect the lifestyle of Sr. Mary in the Nun Study?

2. Have you had any experience with family members or friends who have Alzheimer's disease or dementia? What have you learned about caring for or comforting them?

3. What kinds of things are you doing to ward off dementia?

# CHAPTER 4

# To Retire or Not to Retire

When he was fifty-four, Tom Scherr was told that he would lose his benefits if he didn't retire voluntarily. Tom and his wife, Nancy, had three kids in college, and Tom's mother was living with them. Tom decided to take an advance on his pension to help cover tuition costs and living expenses, even though doing so would ultimately reduce his pension payouts when he retired.

What Tom didn't realize is that within a few weeks, he would land another job. "You make decisions based on the information you have at the time," he says. "There's no sense in beating yourself up. Do I have some regrets? It wouldn't be normal if I didn't have some regrets, but for the most part, I think Nancy and I made good, sound, and prayerful decisions."

Tom worked at the new job for another ten years. When the company offered a retirement incentive, Tom took the offer and says he "danced down the street."

Tom's experience runs the gamut from being devastated at a forced early retirement to being elated ten years later when he was offered a retirement incentive. The decision to retire or not to retire can be complicated.

## Happy about Retirement

Some people have good reasons for wanting to retire and they are happy about it. One high school teacher took advantage of an early retirement incentive. "I had seen a lot of my friends who had started before me get frustrated with the kids or something that happened, and by the time they retired, they were angry," she says. "I didn't want to leave angry. I still loved to teach, but the situation was right, so I took the incentive."

A seventy-year-old woman decided to retire from her job as a rectory housekeeper because "my body was telling me it was time to move on to other things."

People who are happy about retirement talk about the freedom to do what they want to do, opportunities to travel, a chance to learn new things or develop new hobbies, and the joy of being able to sleep until they wake up naturally.

## Unhappy about Retirement

People who are forced to retire find their retirement much more stressful. In fact, retirement is ranked number ten on the Holmes-Rahe Stress Inventory, a measure of the likelihood that different stressful events might cause illness.[12] Retirement is outranked only by heavy-duty stressors, such as the death of a spouse or a close family member, marital difficulties and divorce, imprisonment, personal injury or illness, and getting fired or laid off from a job.

Susan Stout was forced to retire from her position as an administrative assistant for six Catholic parishes when a new pastor was assigned and brought his own staff members with him. "I wasn't prepared to retire and could not imagine what it would look like," she says. "I was petrified. Slowly, but steadily, I adjusted as I pretended I was on vacation for the first month.

Everyone except me was excited about my retiring, especially my friends who were already retired. I am still adjusting to the retirement state of mind. I miss the people I served and the people I worked with. I accepted it, even though I wasn't 100 percent happy."

## Unsure about Retirement

Sometimes people have mixed feelings about retirement. Mark Piscitello is a welder. "I do and I don't look forward to retirement," he says. "In one way I'm looking forward to retiring and seeing where the Lord is going to lead me. But right now, I have it made at work. They are trying to keep me as long as they can because they are so busy."

Beth Mattingly loved being a domestic relations judge, but circumstances indicated it was time to retire. "I was up for reelection," she explains, "and it didn't make any sense to run for another term because I didn't want to work that long. A wise woman once told me, 'The biggest mistake is not retiring too early; it's retiring too late.'"

Looking back, Teri Donner would agree with that statement. She was a paralegal specializing in real estate. During the economic downturn in 2007–2008, the attorney she worked for lost a lot of business, and Teri was laid off. Teri started to look for another job, but her husband, Charlie, pointed out that she would be at the bottom of the barrel in a new law firm in terms of vacation time off. With grandchildren being born and a daughter living out of town, he encouraged Teri to retire. Charlie retired a few years later.

"It gave us time to travel and do wonderful things," Teri says. "Had he not retired when he did, he would have been working until the day he was diagnosed with cancer. So, God works in strange ways."

## The Decision to Keep Working

According to a recent Gallup poll, nearly half of baby boomers say they won't retire until they are sixty-six or older.[13] One in ten say they will never retire. Half of the respondents who plan to continue working genuinely like what they are doing and do not want to stop. Some said their decision was based on their professional goals for the future. Others said working gave them a sense of personal value.

Mary Virginia has no plans to retire. "I am a practicing attorney, and I maintain my own office," she says. "I have managed to carve out a niche for myself in my law practice that I am very happy with. I can work as little or as much as I want, depending on my schedule and financial needs."

Veronica Cavan retired from teaching several years ago, but her husband, Ed, owns his own insurance agency and has no plans to retire. "He has control of his schedule so that he can golf, and we can travel," she says. "It is working for us."

Financial considerations play a big role in why people continue to work.[14] Too much debt, not enough in savings, or the desire for a lifestyle that wouldn't be possible on a fixed income are all factors. A Gallup survey found that baby boomers who "strongly agreed" that they had enough money to do everything they want to do in retirement planned to stop working at sixty-six. Those who "strongly disagreed" with the statement said they would retire significantly later or not at all.

"I have no plans for retirement," says Steven McEvoy. "With the ages of my children and our financial situation, retirement will never be an option. I work full-time in information technology. I have managed computer infrastructure on every continent except Antarctica. Fortunately, working in IT, even if I need to retire from a job because of aging out, I will be able to consult or work on contract as long as I can."

## Easing into Retirement

Some people ease into retirement by moving to part-time work. Marianne Hanley, an attorney, arranged for her full-time legal position in a hospital to be divided into two parts. "I wasn't ready to retire completely," she says. "It was perfect for me. I worked two days a week for the next three years."

Ted Sosnowski worked in finance and administration, but his job was eliminated when he was fifty-seven. After a lot of prayer and a yearlong search, the opportunity arose for a job as a business manager in a Catholic parish. He worked in this position for eight years. When he retired, the pastor at his own parish asked if he would assist the new business manager on a part-time basis. So, Ted did that for a few more years.

"It was a great transition," he says. "By the end of it, I was ready to retire for real."

## Transitions

Some social scientists now believe that retirement should be viewed as a series of transitions rather than a onetime event. How people navigate through retirement transitions depends on a variety of factors, such as health, financial security, job satisfaction, family situations, whether they want to retire or are being forced, and how well they have planned for retirement.

Dr. Nancy K. Schlossberg, a retired professor of counseling psychology at the University of Maryland, has done extensive research on aging.[15] She identified six different ways that people approach retirement.

- **Continuers** keep using existing skills and interests in a modified way.
- **Adventurers** follow their dreams and embark on new endeavors.
- **Searchers** attempt to find their niche by exploring new options in a trial and error process.
- **Easy Gliders** enjoy free time and do whatever they want as each day unfolds.
- **Involved Spectators** care deeply about their former job or profession and stay informed but do not actively engage.
- **Retreaters** disengage for a while to figure out what they want to do. Some disengage permanently and do nothing.

Some people settle into one of these categories and remain there indefinitely. Others move back and forth through several categories. For example, Marianne Hanley was a "continuer" when she cut her full-time legal position by 50 percent. Three years later, she retired and became an "adventurer" by taking a part-time job at J.Crew during the Christmas season. She thought it would be fun, but it turned out to be more pressure than she anticipated. "My retail days are over!" she laughs.

So Marianne became a "searcher" and started to dabble in different things. She went back to school to learn Italian. She also took bridge lessons and started volunteering in an inner-city school. At the same time, she remained an "involved spectator" in the legal profession, and when she was offered another part-time job as an attorney, she accepted it.

## Understanding Why

According to an old saying, there are two reasons a person does something: the "good" reason and the "real" reason. When it comes to making decisions about retirement, it helps to understand your real motivation.

A mentor once told Joe Buscaglia, "When you retire, you close one door and open another." Joe decided one day that he would retire from his position as a high school teacher at the end of the year. "I left and I never went back," he says. "I don't open doors that I have shut."

His wife, Rosemary, worked for three years after Joe retired. She points to the fact that she and Joe grew up with different attitudes toward retirement. "Joe's father couldn't wait to retire, and he didn't do much of anything after he retired," she says. "My parents' philosophy was that you keep working because work is good for you. My parents owned a butcher shop and when my father closed the shop at age seventy-eight, my mother went to work in the deli department at a local supermarket. She used to tell me, 'Don't retire. Work is good for your mind. It's good for your body. It keeps you moving.'"

## Making the Decision

Deciding to retire is a big decision, but it's not carved in stone for the rest of your life. If you retire and you like it, that's great. If you retire and you don't like it, you can decide to do something else.

"When I talk to people who have retired, I ask what they miss," says Deacon Ken Henry. "They tell me they miss interactions with people more than anything else. I rarely hear people say they miss the challenges or the frustrations. My advice to people who are thinking about retirement is to make sure they have something to fill that space in their lives. It's important to be engaged in something. A mind or a body in motion stays in motion. I will eventually retire from my job, but I will never retire as a deacon. I plan on serving as long as I can."

# Something to Ponder

God knows what is my greatest happiness, but I do not. There is no rule about what is happy and good; what suits one would not suit another. And the ways by which perfection is reached vary very much; the medicines necessary for our souls are very different from each other. Thus God leads us by strange ways; we know he wills our happiness, but we neither know what our happiness is, nor the way. We are blind; left to ourselves we should take the wrong way; we must leave it to him.

—St. John Henry Newman[16]

## Questions for Reflection

1. What decisions have you made about retirement?

2. What do you see as the pluses and pitfalls of retirement?

3. What advice would you offer to people who are considering retirement?

# CHAPTER 5

# Planning for Retirement

Mary and Earl Cantwell have been planning their retirement for the past two years. "We always knew we wanted a simple life," Mary says. "After all the years of keeping up with the house and the yard work and cleaning and taking care of everything, we just didn't want to do that when we retired."

Over the years, Earl and Mary enjoyed camping, and they often noticed people driving recreational vehicles (RVs). Mary thought it looked like fun to be able to pack up whenever you want and go someplace else.

They decided that this was the lifestyle they wanted in retirement, so they started planning. They went to RV shows. They did research on the internet. They talked about locations they might want to visit. They wanted warm weather during winter months and to be able to walk to a beach, go swimming, and engage in outdoor activities. They considered the Carolinas, but they decided on Florida. "If we don't like it, we can move to a different place," Mary says.

Mary retired early from her job as a receptionist in a psychiatric center so that she could start getting their house in Buffalo ready to sell. Earl is an attorney and will retire shortly before they leave. The financial aspects of their retirement are set. They bought a truck and picked out their RV, but they won't purchase it until they get closer to their departure.

The Cantwells have also thought about what they will do in retirement. Earl is an avid reader, and he wants to write a book. Mary wants to get involved in volunteer opportunities and meet new people. They both want to travel.

The planning Earl and Mary Cantwell are doing lays a solid foundation for their retirement. "We're very excited," Mary says. "We'll be heading for our biggest adventure ever."

## Making a Plan

Research shows that before they retire, 65 percent of baby boomers have some kind of retirement strategy in place that includes financial considerations and a retirement budget.[17]

When Joe McBride started thinking about retirement, one of his former students, who is a financial advisor, asked if he could look at Joe's finances. He concluded that Joe would be all right in retirement if he didn't change his lifestyle and go crazy with spending. "Before they retire, people have to know where they are financially," Joe says. "Some people want the same lifestyle they had when they were working, but they may need to cut back a little. I never wanted the best of this or that. I brought my own lunch to work. I drove around in my old Ford station wagon for a zillion years. I fixed my own house. Now I'm living on my pension. I try not to tap into my savings. If people are living above their means while they are working, it will be harder for them to live within their means when they retire."

### Talking about the Future

Nancy Scherr agrees that finances are a major concern when you begin planning for retirement, but finances are not the only concern. "There needs to be some good conversation about what the future holds," she says. "You are stepping out into the unknown. Without a plan you can get discouraged."

Talking about retirement can make the transition easier. One of the big issues some people face is unexpected marital problems. If retirement is beckoning, here are discussions you might want to have with your spouse:

- **Dream Together.** Talk about your vision of what retirement will be like. You may have different hopes for the future. Suppose one of you wants to travel and the other wants to golf? Or one wants to spend time with grandchildren and the other wants to start a new business. Talking about dreams and expectations is the first step in working out compromises that can avert an all-out war.

- **Talk about Togetherness.** Unless you work together or own your own business, you probably don't spend all your time together now. There's no need for you to be glued to each other in retirement. There will be things that you want to do together, but it's okay to have separate friends, separate interests, and separate activities.

- **Anticipate Change.** Talk about the ways your lifestyle will change in retirement. Does your retirement budget mean that you will need to cut back on spending? Do you need to talk about changes in household responsibilities—especially if one of you plans to retire and if the other decides to keep working? Anticipating change doesn't mean those changes will actually occur, but it opens your eyes to the probability that your retirement lives will be different from your working lives.

- **Explore Your Feelings.** Openly share whatever concerns and apprehensions you may have about retirement. Maybe you're concerned about giving up your work identity. Or you may wonder how you will fill the extra time. Remember that feelings are just feelings. Don't fall into the trap of judging the other person's feelings or trying to fix them. If you are both open to listening to each other's deepest thoughts, it will strengthen the bond between you.

- **Draw Up a Plan.** Even if you don't totally agree on every aspect of the future, it's important to put together a preliminary plan. A plan like this is never carved in stone because circumstances change, but a plan will give you a blueprint to follow as you build this next stage of your lives together.

While these talking points are targeted toward married couples, the need to talk about retirement applies to everybody. Before making any decisions, explore your options with people you trust.

## Learning More

As you plan for retirement, consider attending workshops and reading books that explore different aspects of retirement. Before he retired from the Internal Revenue Service, Mike Reilly went through training to become a retirement coach. He hoped to one day offer seminars on how to plan for retirement. As it turned out, he never presented any workshops and he never coached anyone else, but the training helped him prepare for his own retirement.

As part of his planning, Mike made a list of things he wanted to do in retirement. His list included: join Rotary Club, write a blog, write the family genealogy, write a book, get involved with the Society of St. Vincent de Paul, teach a class, babysit the grandkids, play golf, attend seminars, exercise at the gym.

Mike has accomplished most of the things on his list. He has also decided that he doesn't like the word "retirement." He thinks it sounds as if you're giving up and stopping. Instead, he made up his own word, "inspirement," because it describes retirement as a time for inspiration, new adventures, and new possibilities.

## Testing Your Plan

While they are still working, some people test elements of their retirement plan by dabbling in new hobbies, joining new organizations, making new friends, or trying new recreational activities. Testing different interests can make the transition to retirement a little smoother.

Bill Horn was still working when he volunteered at his parish to take Communion to residents in a local nursing home. "I was dipping my toe into the water," he laughs. After he retired, the experience inspired him to start what he calls a "caring ministry" in his parish with outreach to people who are sick and homebound.

"Retirement can be a wonderful, freeing time, but I think it needs to be approached thoughtfully," one woman says. "This can be a whole new phase of life, with joys and accomplishments to fill the days. Don't waste these years. Make something good with them."

## Something to Ponder

Accept peacefully whatever you have to do and try to get things done in order, one after the other. If you attempt to do everything all at once or without order, your mind will be frustrated and grow weary and you are likely to be overwhelmed by the pressure and accomplish nothing.

—St. Francis de Sales[18]

## Questions for Reflection

1. In what ways have you prepared for retirement?

2. What aspects of retirement do you still need to explore?

3. What is your biggest concern in retirement planning?

# CHAPTER 6

# Downsizing

Paul and Beth Mattingly have a big house on seven acres of land near Cincinnati. "Figuring out how and when to downsize and prepare for the inevitable older years when we might need more help is a big thing," Beth says.

> We had a workforce of four kids, but they are grown up and gone now, and upkeep is hard. We love our home, but I don't know when the right time is to say we can't do this anymore. If we could find a smaller house that met our needs, that would be great. I would like to downsize before my kids are forced to go through my house and do it for me.

The Mattinglys have decided that they will stay in the Cincinnati area because they have two children who live nearby. "I think it is a mistake not to be near one of your children," Beth says. "If you don't have a relative nearby to help you when something happens, it can be bad."

## Where to Go?

According to the 2019 Transamerica Retirement Survey, 69 percent of respondents said affordability was their number one concern in choosing where to live in retirement.[19] Other considerations included nearness to family members and friends

(49 percent), good weather (45 percent), low crime rate (42 percent), access to health care and hospitals (38 percent), and access to leisure and recreational activities (37 percent).

But there are other factors to consider before you make a move. Would you prefer a freestanding house with a yard for gardening? Or would you prefer a condo where someone else takes care of the outside maintenance? Maybe you'd like what is sometimes known as a patio home—a home that may share walls with similar homes or be freestanding. With a patio home, you often have the option of planting your own small garden, but the homeowners association fee covers exterior maintenance and heavy-duty yard work.

Some people want an age-restricted community with pools, golf courses, clubs, and activities designed for people fifty-five years and older. Thirteen years ago, Frank and Joyce Balanda moved into a community for active older adults in Connecticut. "There are three thousand people here living in condos," Joyce says. "The community has one hundred clubs and a lot of cultural and educational opportunities. There is always something to do. I love it here."

Others prefer to live in a more diverse community with people in all age groups. Teri Donner lives in a patio home. "There are a lot of empty nesters and widows here," Teri says. "But I also have neighbors with children. It's a good mix of people."

Continuing care retirement communities are becoming increasingly popular. In these communities you might start out in a patio home, but you have the option of moving into a senior apartment, assisted living, or a skilled nursing unit if the need arises. Some developers are now building these communities close to colleges and universities so that residents can take advantage of opportunities on campus.

Moving in with one of their children might be an option for some people. Mary Ryan laughs when she tells the story of a woman who stopped her at church recently and said, "I remember a few years ago when we were sitting in the parish library and talking about getting older. Everyone was saying, 'I would never go and live with my kids!' But you said, 'If they ask, I'm going!'" Most of Mary's friends hope to stay in their current home as part of a trend called "aging in place."

## Making Choices

There are pluses and minuses to every housing option. Before you decide to move anywhere, visit the places you are considering, talk to people who live there, and make a list of what you like and don't like about each option. Then discuss the possibilities with family members and friends. Be sure to check with your financial advisor to make sure you can afford to move. Keep in mind that even if you decide to age in place, there may be costs down the road if you need to make modifications to your home.

Rich and Mary Bleyle looked into the modifications they would have to make to their home after Rich was diagnosed with a muscle disorder that made climbing stairs difficult. When it became clear that the cost of renovations was not practical, they sold their house in New York and moved into a large house near Atlanta with their daughter, son-in-law, and four grandchildren. The new house has a bedroom suite and sitting area for Rich and Mary on the main floor.

"We tried to make it feel more like home for us," Mary says. "We put a lot of familiar things around us—furniture, rugs, pictures—so there are a lot of personal touches. It was the best decision, but it was hard."

Here are some of the decisions that other people have made:

• One couple sold their sprawling three-story house in the city and moved to a smaller Cape Cod style home in the suburbs. "It has a bedroom and a bathroom on the first floor, so we don't have to worry about stairs every day," they said. "But it also has bedrooms upstairs if family members or friends come to visit."

• Another couple sold the two-story home where they had raised their children twenty years ago and moved into a ranch-style home. But the laundry area is in the basement, and they are starting to have trouble with the stairs. "Maybe we will have to go to a condo or an apartment someday," they say. "But at this point, we're not ready."

• A divorced woman thought that someday she might want to live in a place where someone else would do the cooking and the cleaning. "And then I was in rehab for a week," she says. "It was a learning experience. I didn't always like the food, and I didn't like the routine. I decided that I am going to stay in my house as long as I can!"

- A widow was living in a big house by herself in Maryland. Her son, who was living in California, decided to move to Maine, so she discussed her situation with him. They agreed she should put her house for sale. "Within three months, I was living in a Catholic senior apartment building in Maine," she says. "I'm on the third floor, right next to the chapel. I'm a Eucharistic minister and a lector. I lead the Rosary twice a week and I also lead the Divine Mercy Chaplet. I have been blessed."

## Selling the Family Homestead

There were moments of laughter and moments of tears when Joe McBride sold the house his family had lived in for thirty-seven years. "After my wife died, I traveled around a lot and stayed with my kids," he says. "Every month or so, I would go back home to check the mail, talk to the neighbors, and make sure there were no plumbing leaks."

Last year a tree fell in the yard during a bad storm, and Joe started to ask himself, "Why am I holding onto this house?" He remembered a Joyce Kilmer poem entitled "A House with Nobody in It" that tells the story of an empty house that should have a family in it, but the house sits alone with a broken heart. Joe decided it was time to sell his house, and his kids agreed it was a good idea.

"It took me a few months to get the house ready," Joe says. "I had one day when the kids came and took whatever they wanted. Another day, my sister-in-law and some friends helped me go through the attic and the closets. Every box we opened was full of memories. But I don't have any regrets. The house sold quickly to a young couple. Now they are going to have a baby, so the house is doing what it should be doing. I feel like the house is having a new purpose."

## Cleaning Out Clutter

Most people agree that the hardest part of cleaning out is getting rid of things with sentimental value that no one else wants. Young people today might not want dining room furniture, china, crystal, sterling silver, and linens. As soon as you begin to think about downsizing, it's a good idea to start weeding things out.

"A friend told me that every time the recycling truck comes by, he takes an armful of paperwork that has accumulated in his house and gets rid of it," one man says. "We have a lot of clutter. I have a file cabinet in my attic that is loaded, so I'm going to start recycling too."

### MOVING IN WITH A RELATIVE

Many people vow that they will never move in with their kids, but you may find that it is your only choice. No one wants to be a burden. No one likes adapting to the household routine of someone else. Blending lives can be challenging, but those challenges can be transformed into opportunities that help everyone involved. Here are some things to consider:

- Think positively about what you have to offer in this situation.
- Don't expect to like everything that other family members do.
- Remember that you are not in control.
- Be grateful that they care enough about you to invite you to live with them.
- Stay out of family quarrels.
- Be honest in discussing issues that impact you directly.

## Something to Ponder

Imagine yourself as a living house. God comes in to rebuild that house. At first, perhaps, you can understand what He is doing. He is getting the drains right and stopping the leaks in the roof and so on; you knew that those jobs needed doing and so you are not surprised. But presently He starts knocking the house about in a way that hurts abominably and does not seem to make any sense. What on earth is He up to? The explanation is that He is building quite a different house from the one you thought of—throwing out a new wing here, putting on an extra floor there, running up towers, making courtyards. You thought you were being made into a decent little cottage: but He is building a palace. He intends to come and live in it Himself.

— C. S. Lewis[20]

## Questions for Reflection

1. In what ways would you like to simplify your life?

2. How would you begin the process of downsizing?

3. If you had to move out of your home, what new living arrangements would you consider?

# CHAPTER 7

# Letting Go

The prayer line at Our Lady of Good Hope Parish in Fort Wayne, Indiana, accepts prayer requests from people who call or email with special intentions. Then the prayer coordinator sends a message to team members who pray for those intentions daily. After coordinating the prayer line for twenty years, Nancy Riecke felt that God was telling her the time had come for a younger person to head up this ministry.

"I prayed about it, talked to a couple of close priest friends, and prayed some more," Nancy says.

There were several people who might be willing to coordinate the prayer ministry, but over and over, the name of one particular woman kept coming into Nancy's mind. When she mentioned it to a priest, he told her this woman was too busy with her eleven children to get involved. But Nancy continued to feel as if God was leading her toward this woman, so she decided to ask her. The woman agreed to take over the ministry.

"She's doing a great job," Nancy says, "and thankfully, she allowed me to remain a part of the prayer team as a consultant and to substitute for her when she is unavailable."

Nancy recognized that the time had come for her to let go. Aware of her age, she knew it was important that someone else take over the ministry so it could continue if something happened to her. "There are still many things I can do to help," she adds.

Whether Nancy realizes it or not, letting go is the essence of authentic spirituality. Once you begin to let go, you allow the Holy Spirit to work through you and lead you in new directions.

## Giving Up Control

Most of us operate under the illusion that we are in control. Sometimes, recognizing that we are getting older shatters that illusion. Like Nancy, we see that it's time to give others the opportunity to do the things that we have always done, and to let them do things in their own way, even if different from our way.

Rosemary Buscaglia struggled with the idea of turning over Thanksgiving dinner to her daughter. "My daughter had just gotten married, and she wanted to have the family Thanksgiving dinner in her new home," Rosemary says. "I wasn't sure I wanted to let it go. My husband, Joe, said, 'Move on, Rosemary. Give Thanksgiving to her. This will be good. You'll see!'"

Rosemary bought the turkey, went shopping with her daughter, and helped her set the table the night before. The day after Thanksgiving, she said to her husband, "I love this! I don't have any cleanup. I'm not exhausted!"

From that point on, Rosemary's daughter has hosted Thanksgiving dinner for the family. Her daughter also has the family Fourth of July and Labor Day parties. One daughter-in-law has taken over the celebration of Mother's Day. The other daughter-in-law hosts Father's Day.

"I'm not ready to give up Christmas, and I don't think my kids are ready either," Rosemary says. "But when they are, if I am at the point where I can't do it anymore, I will give it up!"

**Giving Up Worry**

Most of us realize that worry doesn't change anything. It only creates tension in ourselves and in the people around us. There is truth in the adage that 99 percent of the things we worry about never happen.

Twenty-five years ago, Ellen Zupa was diagnosed with chronic leukemia. Her husband, John, urged her to put all her worries in a box, put the box under the bed, and live her life. John was speaking from experience. When he was diagnosed with diabetes forty years before, doctors had told him that he would probably die within twenty years, but first he would go blind.

"None of that happened," Ellen says. "It's important to remember that health statistics are retrospective data based on what has happened to people in the past. No one can predict the future. Some people with a poor prognosis will outlive the expectation. Others with a great prognosis will die. The important question is not how much time do you have left, but how are you going to live your life in whatever time you have?"

**Giving Up Fear**

Most of the people who contributed to this book identified three main fears related to aging: dementia, disability, and dependence. Many had firsthand knowledge of these things because of their experiences caring for elderly parents.

"I think the difference in our generation is that my grandparents had died by the time I was in kindergarten, so my parents didn't witness this kind of deterioration until they went through it themselves," one woman explained. "Our generation has witnessed all of these things happening to our parents, so in some ways, it's more real and a lot scarier."

But as frightening as these fears are, they might never come to fruition.

- Current statistics from the United States Department of Health and Human Services show only 20 percent of adults over age eighty-five need help with personal care. Only 9 percent of adults ages seventy-five to eighty-four and only 4 percent of adults ages sixty-five to seventy-four need help.[21]

- The prevalence of physical disability in older Americans has also declined according to a 2018 report from the National Institutes of Health, and new interventions are being developed to prevent disability or to help people deal with disabilities.[22]

- A recent study in the Journal of the American Medical Association shows that cases of dementia in people over sixty-five dropped 24 percent from 2000 to 2012. Researchers believe that rising educational levels and better heart health are related to better brain health.[23]

But even if we are destined to experience dementia, disability, or dependence in old age, stressing over it now is not going to stop it from happening. We have to remember that we have had a lifetime of learning how to deal with whatever might happen in the future. There were times when we had memory lapses at age twenty. There were times when we were dependent on someone else at age thirty. There were times when we were sick at age forty or fifty and someone had to take care of us. When we look back, we can see God working in our lives to sustain us at every age. God was with us in the past. God will be there for us in the future.

"My greatest fears about growing older revolve around becoming incapacitated, losing autonomy, and being a burden to those I love," one woman admits. "When these thoughts start nagging at me, I try to put them out of my mind and put my faith in Jesus, in the knowledge that he will help me cope with whatever comes my way."

## THE BREATHING PRAYER

One of the simplest ways to let go of anything that is troubling you is by turning your breathing into a prayer. It works like this:

Close your eyes and take a deep breath. Imagine that God's love is flowing into you, and breathe out fear; breathe in God's love, and breathe out worry; breathe in God's love, and breathe out any tension or anxiety; breathe in God's love, and breathe out anything else that is troubling you. Now breathe in and out for a few minutes, and imagine that God's love is flowing through you.

This prayer can help you calm you down. It can help you fall asleep if your mind is racing. It can help you know, in the depths of your being, that you are filled with God's love.

## Something to Ponder

Take, Lord, and receive all my liberty, my memory, my understanding, and my entire will, all that I have and possess. Thou hast given all to me. To Thee, O Lord, I return it. All is Thine, dispose of it wholly according to Thy will. Give me Thy love and Thy grace, for this is sufficient for me.

— St. Ignatius of Loyola[24]

## Questions for Reflection

1. What are some of the things you need to let go of in your life?

2. Do you find it difficult to let go? If so, why do you think that is?

3. What good things have happened when you have finally let go of something in your life?

# CHAPTER 8

# Reinventing Yourself

A restructuring at her place of employment led Dr. Helen Scieszka to retire earlier than she had planned. Trained as a clinical psychologist, she had worked in private practice, in hospitals, and she had taught college courses. In addition, she had obtained a masters-level certification in theology that qualified her to work in parishes and on a diocesan level.

Helen admitted that she felt some apprehension during the months when she was looking for a new job. "But when a job wasn't forthcoming, there was simply an acceptance and a moving forward with the knowledge that this was just how it was going to be," she says.

Facing an early retirement, Helen had to reinvent herself. She decided to focus on writing short stories and books. Helen's education, her career and life experiences, her national and international travels, her enjoyment of people, her belief that everyone has a story, and her deep love of her Catholic faith are all brought together in her writing. Helen is the same person she has always been, but she has reinvented herself.

## What Does Reinventing Yourself Mean?

To reinvent is to make, as if for the first time, something that has already been invented. When you reinvent yourself, you are still the same person you always were, but the changes you make can give you a new direction in life, help you see yourself in a fresh way, or lead other people to see you in a different way.

One woman is planning to retire after a long career, and she is struggling with the idea of reinventing herself. She acknowledges that she is a wife, a mother, a grandmother, and a businesswoman. "But what does that mean when I leave my job?" she wonders. "I feel as if I am back in the 1960s asking 'Who am I?'"

## Discovering Your Identity

It is important to remember that when we stop working at a job, we are only giving up what we *did*— not *who we are*. This can be a difficult concept to embrace because we live in a world that expects us to accomplish something. But our essential identity is as a person created in God's image—a child of God with gifts and talents, strengths and weaknesses. When we come to the inner recognition of this, we begin to recognize that what we *do* should flow from *who we are*. While we were working, we may have been defining ourselves based on what we did.

Discovering your true identity doesn't happen instantly. Look at the lives of the saints. Most of them went through a transformation of some sort in their lives. Often they experienced a breaking point followed by a time of questions, doubts, and struggles before they finally accepted a new understanding of themselves. With God's help, they reinvented themselves.

Problems arise when people refuse to ask themselves authentic questions about who they are. They give up on life when they stop doing whatever they were doing in their jobs—I'm a manager and I don't manage anymore, or I'm a salesperson and I don't sell anymore. They become depressed or irritable instead of realizing that they have the opportunity to live authentically by becoming more of who they were all along.

## Making a Choice

In some ways, we are like grapes in a vineyard. When we're working, we're ripening on the vine. When we stop working, we're more like grapes that have been plucked and crushed into grape juice. Our essence is still there, but we can't go back to being grapes in the same way. Unlike grapes, however, we can make a choice: we can come through this process as wine, or we can come through as vinegar. We can become better, or we can become bitter. How we reinvent ourselves is always a choice that we make.

Researchers at the University of California at Berkeley proved that it is never too late to reinvent yourself. The Mills Study examined personality traits, social influences, and the personal development of 120 women over the course of fifty years.[25] They found that women between the ages of sixty and seventy had successfully changed themselves in positive ways and had become even more of the person that they wanted to become.

## Building on Pain

Some people reinvent themselves by becoming wounded healers. They recognize that their own painful experiences from the past can be transformed into a way of helping people who are going through similar suffering.

Diane Germain reinvented herself by building on experiences of loss. Today, as part of her parish bereavement ministry, she helps other people who are grieving. "With God's grace, I have overcome losses, as we all do," she says. "I feel that God has called me to be present to people who are grieving—to listen, to pray, to hold, or to hug. I try to put things in God's hands, taking one day at a time, being grateful for the struggles that have taught me compassion and understanding. We are here to help each other and love each other. This is what gives my life meaning and gives me satisfaction in my later years."

Barbara Wyse and Veronica Cavan used their experiences of divorce to help others. They both found spiritual and emotional healing by going through the Church annulment process, and they recognized an opportunity to help others. They received training from their diocese, and now they offer free workshops for people who are seeking annulments. "It has been life-giving," Barbara says. "Meeting people, listening to their stories, and walking through the process with them has made this a real ministry."

There are many other examples of retired people who have transformed their lives as wounded healers. A recovering alcoholic helps other men who are trying to break the addiction. A cancer survivor reaches out to people who have been newly diagnosed. A couple whose daughter struggled with depression and committed suicide became involved with a group that promotes education and support for people with mental illness.

## The Big Picture

If there is a secret to reinventing ourselves, it is the realization that we are part of something bigger than ourselves. We are participants in the great mystery of life. When we begin to see ourselves and other people from this greater perspective, we can't live in the same way that we did before. We are transformed. We have a sense of freedom. We become our true selves.

## Something to Ponder

God has created all things for good; all things for their greatest good; everything for its own good. What is the good of one is not the good of another; what makes one man happy would make another unhappy. God has determined, unless I interfere with his plan, that I should reach that which will be my greatest happiness. He looks on me individually, he calls me by my name, he knows what I can do, what I can best be, what is my greatest happiness, and he means to give it me.
—St. John Henry Newman[26]

## Questions for Reflection

1. In what ways have you reinvented yourself?

2. How did you come to recognize that there is a difference between who you are and what you do?

3. What aspects of yourself did you build on in the process of reinventing yourself?

# CHAPTER 9

# A Sense of Purpose

When Nancy Lowczys' husband, Jerry, was diagnosed with cancer in 2013, she retired early from teaching in a school that was connected to a Catholic mission. After Jerry died, Nancy was offered the opportunity to return to teaching third graders in the school on a part-time basis. "I jumped on it because doing something for those kids gives purpose to my life," she says. "These kids come in with a lot of baggage. But there are so many success stories."

We all need purpose in our lives. A sense of purpose allows us to start each morning with a focus on what we want to accomplish that day. It gives us a sense of meaning and fulfillment. When we have a sense of purpose, we think less about ourselves and more about what is going on around us. When we don't have a sense of purpose, we can become bored, disillusioned, anxious, cynical, and depressed.

In a recent study, researchers at Harvard found that people who have a sense of purpose in life were more likely to remain independent and functioning as they aged.[27] Among other characteristics, people with purpose had a stronger handgrip and a brisker pace of walking, which are indicators of physical strength as people age. Having a sense of purpose in life is also linked to living longer, sleeping better, and having a lower risk of disease.

## Making a List

Every morning, Dianne McMahon makes a list of what she wants to accomplish that day, crossing each item off as she completes it. "It's important to do something every day," she says. "Then you feel like you have purpose in life."

Sometimes Dianne's list is long, but other times, when she doesn't feel like doing much, the list is short. On some days, she lists important items like appointments or volunteering or going out to lunch with friends. On other days, she lists more mundane tasks like going to the grocery store or writing a thank-you note. At the end of the day, Dianne has the satisfaction of seeing that she has crossed off most or all of the items on her list. It gives her a sense of having done something, of having accomplished something.

## A Spiritual Component

There is also a spiritual component to having a purpose in life. As children, we learned in catechism class that our purpose in life is to know, to love, and to serve God in this world, and to be happy with him forever in heaven.[28]

Stop and think for a moment how powerful it can be for a person who enters into this deep understanding of their identity before God. They not only discover God, but they discover their true purpose in this world. Their actions flow from self-understanding and self-awareness. Who they are before God determines what they are doing with their lives.

For example, a ninety-five-year-old woman who can't get out much anymore prays the Rosary every day for friends and relatives. "I may not be useful in the ways I was before," she says, "but I have more time for prayer now. There are so many ways that prayers are needed."

Prayer gives meaning and purpose to the lives of Gary and Kay Aitchison. Gary is a deacon, so he is required to pray the morning and evening Liturgy of the Hours. He and Kay pray the Liturgy of the Hours together, and it has become an important part of their day. "For more than twenty years, we have also spent an hour a week in Adoration," Kay says. "When we retired, we began attending daily Mass. All of this gives perspective and purpose to our lives."

## Using Your Gifts

We find purpose in using our God-given gifts and talents. "God made us who we are, and he wants us to be the best person we can be," says Sr. Marie Schober. "He doesn't want us to try and be someone else. God wants us to use the gifts that we have. That's what gives us happiness, energy, and purpose."

She offers the example of someone who likes to knit. That person can knit clothing or blankets for other people. If you love children, you could tutor first-graders who are learning to read. Some people who love babies spend several hours each day holding sick infants in the hospital.

"If you are disabled, that's going to limit what you choose to do, but it doesn't mean that you can't choose something life-giving," Sister Marie says. "We have sisters who cannot go out anymore, but people come to them to learn English as a second language."

One woman who loves sewing makes quilts for a Ronald McDonald House. A man who loves music leads sing-along sessions at area nursing homes. Some people become foster grandparents for children in need. Others teach adults to read at the local literacy center.

## Inspiring Grandparents

Ken and Marilyn Henry find meaning and purpose in many aspects of their lives. They both work part-time and Ken is also a deacon at their parish in Houston. Their ministry through the Catholic Grandparents Association is another source of satisfaction as they touch the lives of other grandparents.[29]

Ken and Marilyn were on vacation in London when Marilyn found a brochure in Westminster Cathedral about the Catholic Grandparents Association, an international organization dedicated to supporting the vocation of grandparents. When they returned home, Marilyn started a chapter at their parish and recruited Ken to serve as the group's spiritual director. Together they offer spiritual and emotional support for grandparents, along with fun activities for grandparents and grandchildren.

Marilyn's involvement with the organization on an international level has brought her into contact with grandparents all over the world. Today, she is the contact person for anyone wishing to connect with the organization or start a chapter in the United States. Recently, she found a powerful summary of the role that a strong sense of purpose plays in people's lives.

"I was asked to do a talk about the origins of the Catholic Grandparents Association," she explains. "As I was doing research for the talk, I found an African proverb that said, 'Young people know how to run fast, but old people know the way.' I loved it. It was perfect."

## Something to Ponder

God has created me to do him some definite service; he has committed some work to me which he has not committed to another. I have my mission. . . . I am a link in a chain, a bond of connection between persons. He has not created me for naught.

—St. John Henry Newman[30]

## Questions for Reflection

1. What gives meaning and purpose to your life?

2. Can you recall a time when you had to find a new sense of purpose?

3. What benefits come from having a sense of meaning and purpose?

# CHAPTER 10

# A Positive Attitude

Joe McBride says he was born with a "happy gene." He is an optimist by nature, but he also says that he chooses to be optimistic. He isn't sure, however, that optimism is a choice everyone can easily make. "I made that choice. I was given opportunities to do so. But the older I get and the more experience I have, I see that not everyone gets dealt the same deck of cards."

Joe McBride raises some interesting questions: Is optimism an inherited trait? Is it a learned behavior influenced by the way you grow up? Or is it a conscious choice that you make?

The answer might be that positive attitudes are a little of all three.

## The Latest Findings

In a 2011 study involving 326 participants, researchers at the University of California in Los Angeles combined psychological testing with analysis of the participants' DNA.[31] The researchers found that people with a positive approach to life and people with a negative approach had variations in certain genes.

Three years later, a researcher at the University of Edinburgh studied optimism and pessimism in identical twins who share the same genes and fraternal twins who share half of their genes.[32] Both the identical and the fraternal twins also shared the same upbringing in their family environments. The researcher found that although optimism and pessimism have separate, identifiable genetic components, the way a child is raised can also have a substantial impact on whether that person tends to have a positive or negative outlook on life.

The takeaway from these studies is that yes, genes do influence attitudes. But the influence of your parents and other people in your life also helps form the way you look at the world and how you cope with positive and negative emotions. So even if you have a genetic predisposition toward negativity, you can take steps to change your thought patterns in a more positive direction.

## What Is an Attitude?

Attitudes are thoughts or feelings that have become so ingrained that they have become habits. We don't consciously think about our attitudes—we just have them, and they affect how we behave.

"A friend told me that when we turn fifty, we can have a new attitude," one woman recalls. "We have the wisdom to lead healthy, life-giving lives without worrying about others' approval or disapproval. We can feel free to be ourselves."

This woman embraced a positive attitude about herself at fifty, and her positive attitude led her to behave in ways that were self-confident and proactive. But what would have happened if she had adopted a negative attitude? What if had she felt bitter, cynical, or insecure? How would that have changed her outlook on life? How would her negative attitude have changed her behavior?

## Examining Attitudes

If you want to take a closer look at your attitudes, the first step is to take an honest look at yourself. Do you see yourself as basically happy or unhappy?

People who are basically happy look on the bright side of things. They don't internalize bad experiences or expect them to continue. If bad things do happen, they expect that they will be able to deal with them.

People who are basically unhappy look on the dark side. When something bad happens, they see it as another example of the ongoing string of bad situations in their lives or in the world. They don't expect difficulties to end, and they don't feel they can do much to make life better.

If you see yourself as being positive, that's great. Keep being positive! If you suspect that you've fallen into a habit of negativity, take a closer look at self-defeating behaviors that might stem from negative thoughts and attitudes, such as complaining, criticizing, gossiping, stubbornness, and grumpiness. Then try to break the negative cycle.

## Strategies for Change

Here are some techniques for changing negative attitudes and behaviors:

- Ask yourself why you are thinking negative thoughts.
- Ask yourself what would happen if you thought the opposite.

- Tell yourself that bad situations are not permanent. Life will get better.
- Let positive thoughts override negative attitudes.
- Be open-minded. Don't automatically say no to new ideas or opportunities.
- Seek out people who have a positive attitude.
- Choose to do something fun.
- Recognize that it takes time and effort to change negatives attitudes into positive attitudes.
- Be persistent. Keep working at it until you're successful.

One man said he would like to teach a class on optimism. "I don't understand people who just shut down and turn negative," he says. "When bad things happen, you always have a choice. You can give up, or you can pick up the pace. You can't let the bad things get you down."

## Making Positive Choices

"People tell me that I'm a positive person," one woman says. "It is not something that I consciously work at. Like everyone else, negative thoughts pop into my head. If it's a negative thought about another person, I stop myself and say, 'You never walked a mile in their shoes!' The only other negative thoughts I've had are about politics, and I don't dwell on them."

Another woman tells herself to "knock it off" whenever she starts to feel negative. Then she reframes her thoughts to focus on good memories. "We all know people who are so negative that they wallow in it," she says. "But your life is a gift from

God, and how you live your life is your gift back to God. You have to look at the positive."

## Counting Your Blessings

Cultivating an attitude of gratitude is one of the best ways to foster a positive attitude. Dr. Sonja Lyubomirsky, a professor of psychology at the University of California Riverside, says that people who were asked to "count their blessings" as part of a research experiment became happier and healthier, and they remained that way for as long as six months after the study was over.[33]

Without even realizing that she is doing it, Mary Ryan illustrates how an attitude of gratitude can make a difference—even when facing serious difficulties. "We've had some rough spots along the way," she admits. "My husband, Pat, has dementia, and I am the only person he still knows. But we live in our own house, and he is still getting out and doing things. We go for ice cream. We go shopping. He likes to go bowling. He loves going to church."

Last year, Mary was diagnosed with blocked coronary arteries and had stents put in place. Two weeks later, she found a lump that turned out to be breast cancer. This year she needed a knee replacement. She jokes that physically and mentally she is okay from the neck up, and her husband is okay from the neck down!

Mary also talks about how grateful she is for all the good things in her life. "Our children are marvelous about coming whenever we need help," she says. "We have friends who visit. The husband will do a jigsaw puzzle with Pat while I go out shopping with the wife. I feel so blessed. I cannot complain. Pat and I have had a good life and a longer life than many people have had. I count my blessings and I keep my faith. It helps to have faith to hang onto."

Mary Ryan's gratitude for her life despite its difficulties exemplifies the lessons John Leland learned when he spent a year interacting with older people. "The elders were all proof that you could live a full and fulfilling life even when the weather turned stormy. So why worry about the clouds in the forecast? Live your life, put on a show, take a chance, and give thanks for your failures along with your successes—they're two sides of the same coin. If we're living longer, maybe we have an obligation to live better: wiser, kinder, more grateful and forgiving, less vengeful and covetous. All those things make life better for everyone, but especially for the person trying to live by them."[34]

## THE DOWNSIDE TO POSITIVE ATTITUDES

If there is a downside to positive attitudes, it is the increased chance of being taken advantage of by unscrupulous people who target older adults with offers of bogus products and services, false threats about Social Security or Medicare, desperate requests for financial assistance while posing as a family member or friend, "free" gifts or prizes or vacations, and fake charities. Most of these con artists are trying to steal your identity, your credit card information, or your savings.

The FBI says older people are more likely to have savings, to own their home, and to have good credit, which makes them especially attractive to crooks. The FBI also notes that people who grew up in the 1930s, 1940s, and 1950s were raised to be polite and trusting.[36]

When scammers call, text, email, or show up at your front door, this is not the time to focus on having a positive attitude. Government agencies, telephone companies, and internet providers are working to stop scams, but in the meantime, experts advise not to pick up the phone if a number on your caller ID is unfamiliar. Delete text messages or emails from people or organizations you don't know. Don't ever send money or gift cards to someone who says they need immediate help.

Even if you get a message soliciting information from Social Security, Medicare, your bank, or your credit card company and if the formats and logos seem recognizable, it probably isn't legitimate. Be skeptical. Most legitimate institutions will never contact you asking for information or pressure you into answering questions or making a spur-of-the-moment decision. Don't ever give out personal information, financial information, or your credit card number to anyone on the phone or on the internet. When in doubt, don't do anything—even if someone insists that it is an emergency. It is more likely to be a scam.

## Something to Ponder

To be grateful for the good things that happen in our lives is easy, but to be grateful for all of our lives—the good as well as the bad, the moments of joy as well as the moments of sorrow, the successes as well as the failures, the rewards as well as the rejections—that requires hard spiritual work.[35]

—Henri J. M. Nouwen

## Questions for Reflection

1. How would you describe your general attitude toward life?

2. How do you deal with negative thoughts that pop into your head?

3. In what ways have you tried to cultivate an attitude of gratitude?

# CHAPTER 11

# Risk Taking

For twenty years, Joyce Balanda and her husband, Frank, escaped the Connecticut winters and spent four months in a condo on the beach at St. Simons Island, Georgia. On the day they returned home in 2018, Frank died unexpectedly.

Eight months passed, and Joyce debated with herself whether to drive back to St. Simons for the winter. The thought of driving alone and staying by herself in a motel made her nervous. At the last minute, she decided to go.

"I took it easy on the trip," she recalls. "I stayed in motels two nights. I stopped for the day at 2:30 or 3:00 in the afternoon so that I could get settled and get something to eat before it got dark. I felt very vulnerable."

When Joyce was registering at one motel, someone was standing behind her, so Joyce told the woman at the desk she wanted two keys—one for her husband who was in the car. "The last thing I wanted was for someone to know that I was traveling alone," she explains.

Joyce admits that driving over 1,000 miles by herself took guts, but she says it was the best thing she could have done. "St. Simons was a really happy spot for Frank and me," she says. "If I didn't go the year he died, I never would have gone again. I would have lost out on being in the place where we had so many happy memories. I had to take that trip. I think Frank would have been disappointed in me if I hadn't gone."

## Taking Risks

Everyone lives with some element of risk every day. It can be something ordinary like crossing the street or striking up a conversation with someone you've never met before. Or it can be something big like Joyce's decision to drive to St. Simons Island by herself.

You might assume that older people would be more reluctant to take risks. But a recent study by the Max Planck Institute for Human Development found just the opposite was true.[37] Older people tend to make riskier decisions than younger adults. The researchers found that because older people tend to have a more positive outlook on life, they are also more optimistic when faced with risks. When the older respondents in the study weighed the pluses and minuses of their options, they were less worried about possible losses than the younger respondents.

## Benefits for Your Brain

When you take a risk, you consciously choose to move outside your comfort zone. Research shows that breaking through the comfort barrier has amazing benefits for your brain.

A comfort zone feels safe. It makes life seems predictable. But whenever we move out of our regular pattern of living, our brains make new connections and produce new brain cells. In a process called neurogenesis, these new cells grow in the area of the brain called the hippocampus where we assimilate new information, store long-term memories, and regulate emotions.[38]

No one understands the full impact of neurogenesis, but researchers believe that risk taking could play a role in the development of new brain connections and new brain cells. Here are some of the risks taken by people who contributed to this book.

## Living Abroad

Jack and Marianne Hanley took a big risk and stepped outside their comfort zone when they rented an apartment in Rome for ten weeks. They timed their adventure to coincide with the ancient Lenten custom of attending daily Mass at different "station churches" throughout Rome. The Hanleys attended the 7 a.m. Mass every day at the designated church.[39] The station churches custom dates back to the fourth century when people would walk in penitential procession through the streets to different neighborhood churches. The tradition eventually fell out of practice but was restored by Pope St. John XXIII in 1959.

"I definitely felt that moving to Rome for ten weeks was a risk," Marianne admitted. "Once we got into our apartment and got settled in, it didn't seem quite as risky. It was important for me that we had the structure of going to Mass every morning. The night before, we would do some research on the neighborhood where the next church was located and what we wanted to see and do the next day. We fell into a daily pattern."

Jack says he would do it again. "They had the lights on in the churches, and they would open the catacombs underneath the church," he says. "We got to meet a few seminarians. We visited museums, went to different restaurants, and really experienced what it was like to live in Rome. It was great!"

## Making a Move

John DeWolfe visited Hilton Head Island, South Carolina in 1993 and fell in love with it. "You've got to see this place!" he told his wife, Rosemary. They planned a vacation there, and Rosemary jokingly said she would be willing to move there if she saw a Catholic Church, a deer, and an alligator while they were on vacation. She saw all three. So they gave notice at their jobs, sold their house in northern Virginia, packed up a truck, and moved to Hilton Head. "We took a big risk in coming down here," John says. "If we thought about it longer, we might not have done it. But I'm glad that we did!"

John and Rosemary got involved in a parish as soon as they got there. "Having that involvement and getting to know people was a salvation for us," he says. "I was in my late fifties at the time. We were ready to get out of the Washington, DC, area with all the hustle and bustle. It was time to do something and we did it!"

## Walking the Camino

The Camino de Santiago, also known as the Way of St. James, is a network of pilgrim routes that lead to the tomb of St. James in northwest Spain.[40] Bruce Hayden has walked the Camino five times. "But I only completed it three times because I injured myself along the way," he says. "I broke my ankle once, and I broke my finger once."

Blisters, joint and muscle aches, sunburn, exhaustion, and dehydration are some of the other risks that Camino pilgrims face. On each trip, Bruce walked over four hundred miles. But the physical rigors are secondary to the spiritual component of walking the Camino.

"A lot of people pray as they walk," Bruce explains. "There are small chapels along the way, and most pilgrims spend the night in church basements. I like the solitude of walking alone, but I will talk if someone wants to talk. That's the nice thing about the Camino. You might meet someone and talk for a few minutes, but then you go your separate ways."

The routes take pilgrims through small towns with restaurants and stores where they can buy food and supplies. The journey ends at the Cathedral of St. James in Santiago where pilgrims attend Mass, receive a blessing, and ring the bell signaling that they've completed the Camino.

## Family Adventures

Ken and Marilyn Henry walked the Portuguese route of the Camino with their daughter, her husband, their three children, and Marilyn's sister. "It was awesome," Marilyn says. "We didn't do it the true pilgrim way with hosteling. We carried backpacks and walked, but we had our luggage moved from hotel to hotel because several family members have health issues. It was wonderful having the time to talk with my three teenage grandchildren. The kids looked at it as an adventure.

I looked at it as a spiritual journey. If you feel God is calling you in a new direction, it makes it easier to take a risk."

Marilyn is accustomed to risk-filled adventures. She goes to Guatemala every year on a seven-day mission trip to work with Sending Out Servants, a Catholic lay missionary group that sponsors what they call a "ministry of presence" with the indigenous people who live in the mountain villages.[41]

This year Marilyn brought her seventeen-year-old grandson, a quiet boy by nature, who landed in a situation that was very different from his life in America. He experienced a place where wealth is measured in human values. "He seemed to understand," Marilyn says. "He seemed to get into it."

But Marilyn admits that it is always a risk when grandparents expose grandchildren to deeper levels of spirituality—especially teenagers. "Sometimes they wish I wouldn't," Marilyn says. "But I just keep planting seeds of faith and watering them when I can."

**Offering Hospitality**

After their children were grown, Gary and Kay Aitchison moved out of the house where they had raised their family. Their new house had a suite on the lower level that became a place where Kay and Gary offered hospitality to a wide variety of people—some family members and some strangers—who needed a place to live. The experience has definitely moved Gary and Kay out of an established comfort zone.

"You never know who Jesus will bring to your door," Gary says. "During the twenty-four years we have lived in the house, we have had fewer than two years without someone else living downstairs and sharing meals with us."

The first people they sheltered were their son and his family, who were transitioning between jobs and locations. They stayed for two years. Another son and his family came while he was finishing school. Gary and Kay provided a home for several international students who were attending nearby Iowa State University. A grandson came for three months because of a summer job. A young woman came for three years to finish premedical studies. Their oldest son, who never married, lives there now as he recovers from cancer.

"We don't necessarily advocate that people open their homes to others after their families are grown, but we do believe that we are all called to extend hospitality in some way," Kay says. "Being hospitable enriches your life."

Risk taking and moving outside your comfort zone will enhance your life in sometimes unimaginable ways, opening you to possibilities that you might never have encountered. You'll find yourself in contact with people you might not ordinarily meet, and you'll add an element of adventure and fun to your life.

## Something to Ponder

We must learn to live each day, each hour, yes, each minute as a new beginning, as a unique opportunity to make everything new. Imagine that we could live each moment as a moment pregnant with new life. Imagine that we could live each day as a day full of promises. Imagine that we could walk through the new year always listening to a voice saying to us, "I have a gift for you and can't wait for you to see it." Imagine.

—Henri J. M. Nouwen[42]

## Questions for Reflection

1. Describe a big risk that you have taken in your life.

2. What are some of the small risks you have taken?

3. What good things have happened as a result of the risks you have taken?

# CHAPTER 12

# Staying Healthy

Ask Tom and Nancy Scherr what older people need to do to stay physically healthy, and they start talking about balance. "Life is all about balance," Nancy says. "That is an important word for us. People who want to stay healthy need to seek balance in everything they do."

Tom talks about balance in terms of a good diet and regular exercise. "Nancy is better at exercise than I am," he admits. "She goes to the gym three or four times a week, and I go two or three times a week, but we both know it is important. We also like to ride bikes and walk."

Regular exercise also reduces stress, which is a concern for Tom and Nancy. "In this day and age with social media and instant news, we try to balance our use of television," Nancy says. "We find ourselves just turning it off more. We want to know what is happening, but an hour a day is max because otherwise it's not healthy."

Tom and Nancy have identified the key elements that most experts agree are essential to good physical health as people get older. But everyone has a choice about whether or not to put these ideas into practice. Healthy habits won't keep you from aging, but healthy habits can lessen your chance of disease, strengthen your bones and muscles, increase your energy levels, and improve your quality of life.

## You Are What You Eat

Food choices have an impact on your physical health and the quality of your life. The Healthy Eating Plate, created by nutrition experts at the Harvard T. H. Chan School of Public Health, suggests that half of our plate should be vegetables, a quarter of our plate should be whole grains, and the final quarter should be lean protein.[43]

But studies show that as we age, there are physical factors that can affect what we eat, how we eat, and when we eat.[44] For example, we don't need as many calories as we get older because our metabolism slows, but we still have nutritional needs. Taste and smell can also diminish with age and impact our desire for food or lead us to choose the wrong foods. Experts agree that it's a good idea to drink plenty of water and cut back on junk food, fried food, sugary treats, caffeine, and salty snacks.

"I try to cook fresh food and stay away from processed foods," one woman says. "Some days I'm more successful with food choices than other days!" It's also important to remember that changes in body systems can make us feel full more quickly, so we may have to adjust portion sizes. Some people feel hungrier in the morning, so a big breakfast and a light dinner might be a better option.

Drinking too much alcohol can also pose problems for older adults because it increases the risk of falling and causes sleep disturbances. Alcohol can also interfere with the effectiveness of some prescription medications. One couple admitted that their doctor told them to lose weight and to cut back on the amount of alcohol they drink. "It was a real wake-up call for us," they said.

## Keep Moving

People tend to become more sedentary with age, and along with an inactive lifestyle come lower energy levels, problems with balance, difficulty walking, and a greater risk of falling. But these things can often be reduced or alleviated with increased physical activity.

Physical activity has other important benefits. According to the World Health Organization, older adults who are physically active have lower rates of heart disease, high blood pressure, and certain types of cancer. They also have stronger bone health, greater muscle tone, and a better quality of life.[45]

If you're wondering how active you should be, the World Health Organization recommends the following activity levels for people sixty-five and older:[46]

- A minimum of 150 minutes of moderate aerobic activity a week, or 75 minutes of vigorous aerobic activity, or a combination of both.
- Short spurts of aerobic activity that last ten minutes.
- Balance exercises on three or more days a week to prevent falls.
- Muscle-strengthening activities on two or more days a week.

If you can't attain this level of activity, do whatever you can. Walking is one of the best exercises. If you can't walk outside, get up and walk around your house every half hour. If you can't walk to a nearby store, park your car in the farthest parking spot. Moving is good for you!

## Some Good Examples

One woman goes to the gym four days a week. "I do cardio exercise every day on the bike or the treadmill," she says. "Two days a week I do the weight machines. There was a noticeable uptick in my blood sugar levels when I stopped going to the gym last winter. I wasn't losing weight. Since I've started back, I've lost about fifteen pounds."

A seventy-year-old man prefers a men's exercise class at the senior center. "We do some weights, some aerobic exercises, and some resistance exercises," he says. "I've been going for years. I have a lot of friends in the class."

"I am not big on exercise per se," another woman admits. "However, I still mow the lawn, do yard work, and paint the trim on the house. I also enjoy walking."

## Medical Concerns

Do you really need a complete physical once a year? According to a recent AARP report, a complete physical may not be necessary if a person is healthy.[47] Studies show that yearly physicals don't always improve someone's health, and sometimes people are subjected to tests that they don't really need.

As a result, the Society of General Internal Medicine no longer recommends head-to-toe physicals for people who are healthy and have no symptoms.

But that doesn't mean you don't need to see your doctor. Even if you're healthy, it's a good idea to schedule a wellness visit every year or two as a precaution. If you have a chronic condition or are taking medications, you need to be monitored at the frequency recommended by your physician.

It's also important to get an annual flu shot and make sure you're up-to-date with your pneumonia shot. Pay attention to any physical changes you may be experiencing, and bring them to the attention of your doctor. They may be nothing, but if something is going on, it's always better to find out as early as possible.

It is a good idea to maintain a list of your medications, a list of your allergies, a record of surgeries, past medical problems, current conditions, and chronic illnesses. Some paramedics recommend that you keep your list in a place where it can be found easily in case of an emergency.

## Drug Interactions

The older you get, the harder it may be for your system to tolerate certain medications. Every time your doctor prescribes a new medication, ask the doctor or your pharmacist about possible drug interactions that might change the effectiveness of the drug or produce unexpected side effects. It's important to be alert to side effects from over-the-counter medicines as well as prescription drugs.

One woman discovered how devastating side effects can be when her mother was hospitalized after bypass surgery. When her mother came out of the anesthesia, she was very confused. One doctor thought it was loss of oxygen during the surgery. A psychiatrist thought it was Alzheimer's. But the confusion abruptly ended when a drug that had been prescribed after surgery was discontinued. No one had noticed that one of the side effects was hallucinations.

Another woman admitted that she wrestled with the question of side effects when her primary care physician suggested that she might want to take a cholesterol lowering drug even though she didn't have high cholesterol. Studies showed that the drug decreases the risk of stroke among people in her age group. "For people with high cholesterol, I get it," she says. "But I'm at high risk for a stroke because of my age, not because there's anything wrong with me. I've read articles saying some of these studies are too heavily weighted in terms of age, so I am not going to take the drug. As we get older, I think we have to weigh these things more carefully."

## Something to Ponder

Do you not know that your body is a temple of the Holy Spirit within you, which you have from God? You are not your own; you were bought with a price. So glorify God in your body.

—1 Corinthians 6:19-20

## Questions for Reflection

1. How do you take care of your health?

2. How have your exercise and eating habits changed as you've grown older?

3. What advice about staying healthy would you offer to someone else as they age?

# CHAPTER 13

# Friends

Beth Colon and Nancy Lowczys have been friends since first grade. "Our lives were so similar for so long that we could always relate to each other," Beth says. "Throughout the years, even though we've changed in different ways, we still know the core person and that makes our friendship really valuable. I've made a lot of friends through the years in my travels and my jobs, but they always came in at different stages in my life, whereas my early life is unknown to them. There are times when I just don't want to go through all of that and explain who I am. With Nancy, I don't have to do that."

Nancy agrees. "My friendship with Beth means the world to me," she says. "When you have an old friend, that person can go in and out of your life, but when they come back, the relationship is unquestioned, and it doesn't matter that they were absent for a while. You know they are always there if you ever need them or they ever need you."

Beth and Nancy bring different strengths to their relationship, which cements the bond between them. "Nancy is a very gentle person," Beth explains. "I'm not a gentle person, and I need gentle people in my life."

Nancy sees Beth as someone who has always accepted her just the way she is. "I'm on the shy side," she explains. "That's my personality. Beth is one of five friends that I know I can count on. If I didn't have Beth as a best friend, I would be a very lonely person."

## The Power of Friendship

Two recent studies at Michigan State University show that friendships are especially important as people get older.[48] The first study found that among older adults, friendships had a bigger impact on health and happiness than family relationships. The second study showed that when friendships caused stress, participants experienced more chronic illnesses, but when friendships were a source of support, participants were healthier and happier.

As people age, friendships become a safeguard against isolation and loneliness, especially for people who no longer have a spouse or for people who are geographically separated from family members.

## Multiple Friendships

Barbara Wyse has been friends with Veronica Cavan for over twenty years. "She is someone who is there for me, especially since most of my family is out of town," Barbara says. "She understands me. I can tell her anything."

Veronica is Barbara's best friend, but she is not her only friend. "When someone asks me what I like to do, I tell them it depends on which group of friends I'm with," Barb explains. "I go to Mass and out for breakfast with my church group. I golf with a group of retired police officers. I have friends that I used to work with and friends I used to play softball with. I coordinate RCIA in my parish with people who are thinking about becoming Catholic. They are searching, and they have lots of questions. They become friends because of the spiritual journey that we share."

Like Barbara, Mike Reilly has multiple friendships. With some groups he takes a leadership role. With other groups his involvement centers on sports or social activities. For several years, he has been helping a diabetic buddy with memory problems keep track of bank accounts and bills. One day, Mike stopped to see him, and the friend couldn't remember if he had given himself insulin. Mike called his friend's doctor, and the friend ended up in the hospital. When it became clear that the friend could not go back to living alone, Mike helped him move into assisted living. "It's sad," he admits. "But he's my friend, and I do whatever I can to help him."

## Reconnecting

When Tom and Nancy Scherr were in Florida over the winter, they had the opportunity to reconnect with a couple who were in their wedding party. "It was really wonderful," Nancy says. "We hadn't seen these people for a number of years because we had moved out of town, and suddenly, we were back together, and it was amazing. We just picked up again because we left on good terms. Now we can continue to grow in that relationship."

One of the best parts of reconnecting with old friends is reminiscing about the good old days. These kinds of conversations have positive benefits for your brain. A study at Rush

University Medical Center found that when you share happy memories, your brain releases dopamine, a feel-good hormone that lifts your spirits and makes you feel great all over.[49]

## Mutual Support

One woman expressed gratitude for her group of eight women friends. "We laugh a lot about getting older," she says. "We golf and we joke about being on the back nine in terms of our age! Laughter is so important." But they are serious when it comes to the issues of aging. "We talk about how your personality traits become magnified as you grow older," she says. "Sometimes, a great trait—like attention to detail—can become not so great if you start to get picky. We made a pact that if something like that happened to us, we would stop each other."

They also support each other emotionally. Two of them have lost their husbands and said they never would have survived without this group of friends. "Some of us have had other difficulties in life, but having a group in which you can talk and share these burdens really helps."

Her children live out of town, and they want her and her husband to move closer to them. "I told them we can't move because our support system of friends is here," she says. "I want to keep those friendships strong."

## When Friends Aren't Really Friends

One woman has learned over the years that not all people who say they are a friend really are. "Friends become friends for different reasons, at different levels, and at different stages in a person's life," she says.

A man acknowledged that maintaining friendships takes effort and nurturing. "If you don't call someone or write or have lunch or visit, then how can you expect to keep a friendship alive?" he asks. "I have maintained contact with some friends for over thirty-five years. Even if we don't see each other often, it is always a joy getting an email."

Another man admitted that he does not have a lot of friends. "I have a lot of acquaintances," he says. "But the friends I do have mean a great deal to me. And I would do almost anything in my power to help them if they needed me."

## Something to Ponder

One of the most important choices is the choice of the people with whom we develop close intimate relationships. We have only a limited amount of time in our lives. With whom do we spend it and how? That's probably one of the most decisive questions of our lives.

—Henri J. M. Nouwen[50]

## Questions for Reflection

1. How would you describe your friends and your friend-ships?

2. What kinds of things do you do to maintain friendships?

3. How have your friends been an emotional support for you?

# CHAPTER 14

# Learning Something New

Veronica Cavan always wanted to play the piano. About five years before she retired from teaching, one of the other teachers at her school remarried. They had two pianos, and they needed a set of bunk beds, so Veronica swapped her bunk beds for one of their pianos.

"I didn't touch that piano for ten years," she admits. "Then I saw a commercial on television with an actor dressed as Beethoven playing the piano. The voice-over said Beethoven didn't sound that way when he started, and the scene cut to a child playing 'Heart and Soul' with one hand. I don't even remember the product they were selling. The message that stuck in my head was this: everyone needs to start somewhere."

This commercial provided the impetus Veronica needed to sign up for piano lessons. She started taking group lessons and eventually moved to private lessons. She says it was daunting at first. "I remember the first time I had to play chords! I thought, 'Excuse me. You want me to use my left and my right hand at the same time?' It was tough to figure out all those notes, but now I don't even think about it."

Veronica makes it clear that her piano playing is something she does for herself. "You're not going to get a concert!" she laughs. "I won't even do a recital! I like to play because it relaxes me. I really enjoy it a lot."

## Strengthening Your Memory

A recent study funded by the National Institute on Aging found that sustained engagement in learning a new skill enhances memory function in older adults.[51] For three months, participants in the study spent fifteen hours a week learning a demanding new skill. Tests showed their cognitive skills had improved over the course of the fifteen weeks, documenting that learning something new is good for your brain.

One man took up woodworking. "I still consider myself an apprentice with two years of experience. Doesn't it take eight years to be an expert?" he laughs.

An eighty-five-year-old woman attends classes on a variety of topics. "I love every minute of it," she says. "I have learned so much in the past few years. It has helped me to have more confidence and to join in on discussions."

A seventy-year-old woman started taking guitar lessons after her son gave her a guitar as a Christmas present. "I learned enough that I can play," she says. "I am not great at it, but I enjoy doing it. It's a stress reliever. I have a lot of folk songs and hymns that I like playing. Music has always been important to me."

## Learning Together

Beth Mattingly and her husband, Paul, embarked on a new learning adventure together that is both physical and mental. They were watching *Heartland*, a Netflix series about a young girl who helps troubled horses. The more they watched, the more fascinated they became, and one evening Paul said, "We should take horseback riding lessons!"

Beth loved the idea. A vocational school nearby had an equine center that offered lessons. "We took two seven-week sessions and learned about horse anatomy, how to saddle and bridle, how to clean stalls, and how to ride," Beth says.

They're now taking lessons with an instructor who is teaching them more advanced techniques in how to control a horse. "Paul has visions of riding across the range someday," Beth laughs. "It has been a lot of fun, and it is something new that we can learn together."

## Tracing Family Roots

Genealogy is a challenging way to learn something new about your family history. Exploring old records, visiting cemeteries, documenting family stories, and organizing the information so that it makes sense keep the neurons in your brain firing.

Kay Aitchison has worked on her family history for years. She researched and wrote a narrative history of the family and gives a copy to each grandchild when they graduate from high school. She gives each grandchild a copy of the family tree when they get married because they are starting their own branch of the tree. Recently, she has become even more involved in ancestry.com and other online resources.

"I wrote a children's story about my great-great-grandmother who came to the United States from France as a child," she says. "My seventeen-year-old granddaughter is quite a good artist and has agreed to illustrate it. We are hoping to have it bound so we can give it to everyone in the family for Christmas."

Kay believes that learning new things is essential. She and her husband live near a university and take advantage of the educational and cultural opportunities available to them there. "If you are so inclined, join the local community theater," she suggests. "Volunteer as a docent at a museum or art gallery. Go on travel tours to places of interest. Keep learning and growing!"

## Road Scholar

Joyce Balanda combines learning and travel through Road Scholar, an organization formerly known as Elderhostel.[52] Founded in 1975, Road Scholar offers noncredit courses, inexpensive lodging, and interesting excursions for older adults throughout the United states and in 150 countries worldwide.

Joyce has participated in twenty-one trips in the United States. She took several tours in New England, a trip to Maryland's Eastern Shores, a Civil War excursion in South Carolina, a visit to Jekyll Island off the coast of Georgia, an excursion to Mackinac Island off the coast of Michigan, and a trip to San Antonio, Texas.

"The knowledge that you gain is amazing," Joyce says. "The instructors live in the area, and they introduce you to things you might never discover if you were traveling on your own. We did a trip to Maine, and one of the instructors was a professor from Dartmouth. You meet so many interesting people. It's a good way to travel, and it's fairly inexpensive."

## Checking Out Options

Several people extolled the opportunities offered at local senior centers. "Everybody who goes there had jobs and life experiences before they became a senior," one woman says. "There are discussion groups about politics, photography, knitting and crocheting, crafts, starting a business, and figuring out your finances, as well as exercise groups and language groups. It is a good place to join for learning and for socialization. They also have counselors there if you need to talk about something that's going on in your life. It's an amazing place."

Other options for classes and continuing education include museums, libraries, community colleges, and your local school district.

Another great way to combine learning and fun is to join a book club. One woman belongs to three. "One in Florida where we stay for three months in the winter," she says, "a book club with people from the school where I worked, and a third book club during June, July, and August with a nice group of women near our summer home."

## Learning about Faith

When you are checking out options for classes, seminars, and lectures, don't forget about your diocese and your parish. Continuing faith formation for adults is an important part of the mission of the Church.

Through their involvement with the Catholic Grandparents Association, Ken and Marilyn Henry see a great desire on the part of older adults to learn more about their faith. "Now they have time to attend a Bible study," Ken says. "One of the ladies in our grandparents group is just finishing up training in spiritual direction. Several people in our group attend classes taught by a theologian on Tuesday nights."

Emphasizing the importance of ongoing adult education in the faith, Marilyn adds that "we should try to learn something new every day."

One woman started participating in Bible studies when she was fifty. "My faith came alive for me," she says. "The more studies I did with others, the stronger my faith became. I have learned to go deeper into my faith every year. I have learned to trust God in all things, and that has made all the difference. I will continue with my studies until I can no longer physically or mentally participate."

Another woman likes to purchase the booklets and pamphlets that are available in the back of churches. "They have sayings that I cut out and carry in my pocket. I read them when I am walking. One of them was 'Lord, open my eyes and help me to see.'"

## Something to Ponder

If something is true, it is good and it is beautiful; if something is beautiful, it is good and it is true; if it is good, it is true and it is beautiful. And together these elements make us grow and help us to love life, even when we are unwell, even amid difficulties. True education makes us love life, and it opens us to the fullness of life!

—Pope Francis[53]

## Questions for Reflection

1. What new learning experiences have you had?

2. In what ways have new learning experiences changed the way you think or the things you do?

3. What are some new things that you would like to learn?

# CHAPTER 15

# The Joy of Laughter

Diane Germain retired at age fifty-eight. "I thought I knew exactly what I wanted to do," she says. "I wanted to take care of our grandchildren."

Diane babysat for a while, and while she enjoyed spending time with the kids, she also felt that something was missing. Then a friend from her parish invited her to get involved in clown ministry, and a whole new world of fun opened for Diane. She realized that an important part of her retirement was offering the gift of laughter and lightheartedness to others.

Diane developed her own clown costume and identity. She is known as "Bow," short for rainbow, because she has always seen rainbows as an affirmation that God will always be there for her. The clowns visit nursing homes once a month and perform an hour of interactive activities that are designed to amuse and entertain the residents. "They love it, but we each get so much more back," Diane says. "Sharing smiles and hugs is a gift. Being a clown for God is humbling, yet life-giving."

Laughter also has significant health benefits for the clowns and their audiences. Laughter increases oxygen levels and stimulates the heart, lungs, muscles, and circulation. It reduces stress, lowers blood pressure, and makes people feel more relaxed. In the long term, laughter helps to strengthen the immune system, relieve pain, connect with others, and feel happier.

## Sharing Laughter

Caren Kolerski grew up as a perfectionist with no sense of humor. "Every mistake I made was a tragedy," she admits. As an adult, Caren kept thinking that there had to be a brighter outlook on life. She started to pray, "God, lighten me up. Just lighten me up." Her prayer was answered when a friend invited her to attend a school of laughter where she learned a method for bringing laughter into everyday life.

Caren learned how to laugh and has shared her new skills as a certified laugh leader with nursing home residents. "The more I was trying to help other people, I was really helping myself," she admits.

Mike Reilly has taken a different approach. He decided to start a blog for family members and friends "to inject humor into life, to tell about events, and sometimes to write a little philosophy." He frequently finds ways to laugh at his own foibles.

In one of his recent posts, he recounts how he watched his grandsons playing catch with a football one evening. That night, he dreamed that he was playing linebacker, and he intercepted the ball on the goal line.

"Just as I reached the goal line, a swift receiver from the other team dove at me," he wrote in his blog. "I twisted to elude his tackle, and . . . I fell out of bed! Mattresses and box springs are very high nowadays. In addition, I left the drawer in my bedside dresser a bit open. Of course, I caromed off it too. Landing on the floor, I first thought that I'd never survive. I immediately assessed any possible bruises. Head was okay. Arm was scraped, but both legs were hurting. Hence a new football injury. My doctor advised me not to tell anyone. But I told everyone I met!"

## A Sense of Humor

Deacon Tom Scherr says the ability to laugh is essential as people get older. "I think you need to keep a sense of humor," he says. "I try to pull out a humorous remark sometimes. Finding something to laugh about is a way of dealing with the darkness of life. It's important to not take ourselves too seriously."

Pope Francis' sense of humor is one of his most endearing traits. "Christian joy is usually accompanied by a sense of humor," he wrote in his Apostolic Exhortation *Gaudete et Exultate* (On the Call to Holiness in Today's World). "We see this clearly, for example, in St. Thomas More, St. Vincent de Paul, and St. Philip Neri. Ill humor is no sign of holiness" (126).

## The Benefits of a Smile

Studies show that people who smile frequently are thought of as being friendly, helpful, kind, and competent. Smiling offers the same physical and emotional benefits as laughter because it releases hormones in your brain that reduce stress and make you feel happier.

Like laughter, smiles are also contagious. A smile almost always results in someone else smiling back, which produces in them the same positive feelings that the original smiler experiences. St. Teresa of Calcutta understood this simple dynamic. "We give most when we give with joy," she told the Missionary

Sisters of Charity. "If you have difficulties in your daily life, accept them with joy, with a big smile! In this, others will see your good works and glorify the Father."[54]

When asked what advice he would offer to others, Fr. Paul Sabo says, "Remember that the Lord loves you and smile a lot!"

## MAKING YOURSELF HAPPIER

Here are some simple ideas for how to laugh and smile more:

- Make a conscious effort to smile at people, even those you meet in passing.
- Seek out people who like to laugh.
- Make a mental note of all the funny things that happen during the day.
- Bring humor into conversations whenever appropriate, with a funny observation or a joke.
- Make it a point to laugh at other people's jokes.
- Laugh at yourself.
- Remind yourself to lighten up if you find yourself getting negative.
- Get into the habit of laughing every day—even if it is fake laughter. Eventually, laughter will become a normal part of your life.

## Something to Ponder

Grant me, O Lord, good digestion, and also something to digest. Grant me a healthy body, and the necessary good humor to maintain it. Grant me a simple soul that knows to treasure all that is good and that doesn't frighten easily at the sight of evil, but rather finds the means to put things back in their place. Give me a soul that knows not boredom, grumblings, sighs and laments, nor excess of stress, because of that obstructing thing called "I." Grant me, O Lord, a sense of good humor. Allow me the grace to be able to take a joke and to discover in life a bit of joy, and to be able to share it with others.

—St. Thomas More[55]

## Questions for Reflection

1. How important is laughter in your life?

2. What do you do to cultivate your sense of humor?

3. Have you learned to laugh at yourself? In what ways?

# CHAPTER 16

# Giving Back

Kathleen Steigauf spends winters in a senior living community on Hilton Head Island, South Carolina. She plays golf and tennis and takes advantage of a wide variety of "plays, movies, and every kind of club or game you can imagine," she says. But Kathleen also has a deep desire to help others who are less fortunate.

"We have an organization called Staying Connected," she says. "It's neighbors helping neighbors. I volunteer in transportation, and I drive people to appointments and grocery shopping. I find that driving for groceries is more of a social event for some as they can become rather housebound. I think I enjoy it as much as my passengers."

Kathleen also answers the help line for the Society of St. Vincent de Paul in her parish. "People call in when they need financial help with rent or utilities," she explains. "I take as much information as I can regarding the situation. Then I pass that information on to other St. Vincent de Paul members who take it from there."

She is also involved in a group called Second Helping. They pick up day-old bakery items and ripe produce from stores and transport it to food pantries. And she volunteers with a group that packs and distributes bags of groceries for minimum-wage workers.

"There are hundreds of volunteer jobs available," she says. "You don't have to have a special skill—I certainly don't. You just need the desire to pass on what you have. You will get much more back than you give."

## Getting Involved

Deacon John DeWolfe, who works as a pastoral minister at Holy Family Catholic Church on Hilton Head Island, misses snowbirds, like Kathleen, when they go back north for the summer. "We rely on our snowbirds," he says. "They come back every year, and we get them involved in all of our ministries."

Bill Horn, who coordinates outreach ministries at St. William Catholic Church on St. Simons Island, Georgia, warns snowbirds not to be discouraged if someone in a parish tells them they don't need their help. Even in the best parishes, longtime parishioners can get so locked into one way of doing things that they miss the opportunities to include someone new. "If that happens, talk to someone else," Bill says. "We need to find ways to funnel newcomers into existing ministries or spin off into something new."

Bill's wife, Maureen, agrees. She heads up the Society of St. Vincent de Paul in their parish. They reach out to people in need, many of them single moms and children in the nearby coastal city of Brunswick, Georgia, who are okay until their car breaks down or one of the kids gets sick, and then suddenly, they can't pay their rent or their utility bill. "We couldn't help as many people as we do without volunteers," Maureen says. "There is a place for everyone."

## Seeing Christ in Others

In the Gospel of Matthew, Jesus says that when we do something for the least of our brothers and sisters, we do it for him (see 25:31-46). This is Bill Horn's motivation for reaching out to people in need. Bill remembers the first time he recognized the face of Christ in someone else. He was helping to rebuild a devastated community in Mississippi after Hurricane Katrina. "I remember one guy who came to us for help," Bill said. "He had a carload of kids, and he was just trying to survive. I could see Our Lord in him."

The experience stayed with Bill, and now he looks for the face of Christ in the people he visits in nursing homes and the hospital as part of the parish caring ministry. He says one of the most important parts of his ministry is listening. "Once we step into someone else's world, we get their story, and the story helps us to understand what is going on with them," he explains. "Then we can take it a step further and ask how we can help them. Most people just need to talk. They appreciate it when someone listens."

## Reaching Out

Mark and Debbie Piscitello decided to reach out to others after attending a social justice seminar in their parish. At the time, Mark says his faith was all spiritual. "I forgot the human side of Christ and the need to reach out to the poor," he admits. "The speakers opened my eyes. I realized faith is not just me sitting in a room and praying."

A short time later, Mark saw that a Catholic homeless shelter was looking for volunteers. He and Debbie started to volunteer one Saturday a month. They helped with people's clothing and other needs. They served dinner. But mostly they just listened.

"I learned that we are all human," Mark says. "But for the grace of God, any one of us could end up on the streets. I learned compassion and mercy. We were not there to judge these people. We were there to treat them the way Jesus would treat them. Now I see Jesus in everybody."

Whenever we reach out to others, we awaken in those people their giftedness and their dignity, but we also awaken those things in ourselves. We become aware of the reality of God's grace.

## Finding the Right Fit

Dr. Helen Scieszka, a retired therapist, acknowledges that finding the right volunteer opportunity can be challenging. She currently serves on an advisory board for the Aging and Disability Resource Centers in Wisconsin. She also does some writing for a local organization's newsletter. She says volunteering is a wonderful way to meet and interact with people who all have the same goal of making a community better, whether that community is a parish, town, or a nonprofit organization that reaches out to people in need.

"One thing to be aware of is overcommitting yourself," she warns. "There are people who simply love to volunteer for everything, and that's fine. But if you are one who wants to do just some volunteering so that you have time to do other things, then be careful. Be aware of your interests and your skills so that everything matches up. But also, be aware of when you need to say, 'I'm sorry. I can't do that.'"

## The Benefits of Volunteering

A recent study by the Rotman Research Institute show that volunteers over age fifty get more than good feelings from their volunteer work.[56] They also get physical benefits. The results of the research showed that

- older volunteers have less depression, better health, fewer physical limitations, and greater longevity;
- volunteers had less hypertension and fewer hip fractures than people in the control group who did not volunteer;
- people with chronic health conditions benefited the most from volunteering; and
- feeling appreciated or needed boosted a person's feelings of well-being.

"I think everyone should volunteer for something," one woman says. "It helps keep you active. Sitting around doing nothing is, in my opinion, like signing your death warrant!"

"Volunteering, whether you are still employed or not, is important. It allows you to give back for the blessings you have received," another woman observes.

## The Desire to Volunteer

When Vicki Kaufmann was a little girl, she would stop on her way to and from a nearby park and read a public marker by the side of the road:

"I shall pass through this world but once. If therefore, there be any good thing that I can do to my fellow human being, let me do it now. For I shall not pass this way again."

"I must have internalized this message, for it became, along with the tenets of my Catholic faith, my life's calling—a life of service on behalf of those in need."

Over the years, Vicki has worked as a teacher, the director of a family retreat center, and the director of the Catholic Charities office in a rural community. This last job grew into the opportunity to head up social services for Catholic Charities in a large archdiocese. "The last six years before retirement, I directed a department within an ecumenical international relief agency, raising funds for projects to benefit the poor in the Caribbean and Latin American regions," she says.

The main lesson Vicki has learned over the years is that God has been a constant companion on her journey, giving her the strength to forge ahead. She knows that in her retirement years, new paths will open before her and that God will be present to lead and guide her as she continues to reach out to others.

## Something to Ponder

Lord, make me an instrument of your peace:
where there is hatred, let me sow love;
where there is injury, pardon;
where there is doubt, faith;
where there is despair, hope;
where there is darkness, light;
and where there is sadness, joy.

O Divine Master, grant that I may not so much seek
to be consoled as to console,
to be understood as to understand,
to be loved as to love.
For it is in giving that we receive,
it is in pardoning that we are pardoned,
and it is in dying that we are born to eternal life.[57]
                    —The Peace Prayer of St. Francis of Assisi

## Questions for Reflection

1. What kinds of volunteer opportunities are you involved in?

2. What are the benefits you have received as a result of volunteering?

3. In what ways have you seen the face of Christ in other people?

# CHAPTER 17

# Stages of Faith

When Barbara Andrulis thinks about her childhood faith, she remembers "Latin Masses, strict rules, memorizing *Catechism* questions, and images of an all-powerful, punitive God." After the Second Vatican Council, Barb's faith experience began to change. "Mass was now in English," she says, "meatless Fridays occurred only in the Lenten season, and God seemed less harsh to me."

But as Barbara grew into adulthood, there were other changes. She married, moved away from her hometown, and experienced the death of her father when she was in her thirties. These life experiences led Barbara to the realization that she needs God.

"In adulthood, God evolved into a good, reliable friend who was always there for me," she explains. "Prayer wasn't a mandatory set of words but, instead, a conversation with God. I talk to him every day. Some conversations are about gratitude for the blessings in my life. Some are petitions for help, and some are just hello and I'm glad you are around. Sometimes, I ask for one thing and receive another, but I know it is in his plan for me."

What Barbara is describing are the stages of faith that she has moved through in her life.

## How Faith Develops

There are several theories about faith development, but all of them include three important stages:

- **Childhood Faith:** This is a simplistic faith without any room for doubt. Children accept the religious beliefs and practices that their parents pass on to them. They see themselves as being Catholic in the same way they are Irish or Polish or Italian or Mexican. Faith is connected to their family, their heritage, and their culture. There is no personal ownership in childhood faith. It is an extension of what a family believes.

- **Questioning Faith:** During teenage years and young adulthood, questions and doubts arise. During this transition stage, young people let go of childhood faith so that they can grow into an adult relationship with God. Young people sometimes feel alone, confused, and angry in this stage. Some people get stuck in this transition and live in a constant state of questioning and doubt.

- **Committed Faith:** In this stage, adults establish a personal relationship with God and make a mature commitment to faith.

One woman admits that she has just started to recognize the dynamics of her changing faith. "I think I am experiencing a spiritual deepening," she says. "During my childhood and most of my adult years, I practiced my faith out of a sense of tradition and because I wanted to set a good example for my children. Now, I do it for me, and I think I am getting so much more out of it. When people would speak about a personal relationship with Jesus, I don't think I appreciated what they were talking about. But I think I'm starting to understand that this is really the whole point of faith. I try to attend Mass daily, and when I do, I always pray, 'Help me to live like you did, Jesus.' I think this is the purest prayer I have ever uttered, and I strive to really mean these words and to live them."

Another man says that his faith has evolved over time. "In my late teens and twenties I had a very passionate and fiery faith, but I was always jumping from one thing to another," he explains. "Now my faith has deepened. With a focused and intentional goal of reading good Catholic books each year, my faith is more rooted and firmer. My faith has a form and structure now but is still fluid enough to allow for change and growth. My Catholic faith has become more core, more central to who I am. It has helped to balance out some of the rougher edges from my youth, teens, and early adulthood."

## Looking Back

Pope Francis recommends looking back on our faith experiences throughout the years as a way to recognize how far we have come on our spiritual journey. "Each of us has moments such as these: when I got to know Jesus, when he changed my life, when the Lord showed me my vocation, when the Lord visited me at a difficult time," he says. "We all have these moments in our hearts. Let's contemplate them."[58]

When one woman looks back, she sees how much stronger her faith has grown with passing years. "Challenges come with living and at some point, it became clear to me that I couldn't manage everything on my own," she says. "I still did the best I could in every situation, but I realized that I needed to cling to the Lord more and more. I gave things over to him in faith, knowing that he would be my friend, my guide, and my sustenance."

Another woman agrees. "God has ways of pulling us back into his arms," she says. "There was a time when I didn't realize that God was always there for me. I thought if he wasn't answering my immediate prayers with the answers I wanted, he wasn't listening. Now I know he has always been there and continues to be there for me, but it took aging to realize this. Today, my prayer life is stronger—not perfect, but I know he is listening, and I know he knows I am trying. I have learned that prayers are answered in God's time, not mine, and I have to trust. I am more at peace with his plan, and I accept that some of my prayers may never be answered in my lifetime."

## How Prayer Changes

When we look back, we can also see the ways our prayer experiences have changed over the years.

"My prayer has definitely changed as I have gotten older," one man says. "I now have a real relationship with Jesus. I do more listening and less talking. Prayer is simpler. If I am reading Scripture and some thought touches me, I think okay, the Lord is speaking to me. Maybe nothing comes to me, but I still know the Lord is here with me. I am more trusting with the Lord. I can talk to the Lord about anything and wait to see where it leads. One way or another, in God's time I get an answer."

Another man finds that he prays more often. "I pray in different ways throughout the day," he says. "When I'm in the car, I often pray for people and situations I know about. I also have email reminders for numerous prayers throughout the day, from a prayer before using the internet in the morning to an examination of conscience at night. I pray outside of these reminders, but the reminders help me to be intentional. For example, a friend recently asked for prayers for three things. I set up an email notification for every day at 5 p.m. and I say three Hail Marys for him. I will pray them until my friend says they are no longer needed."

## Praying Together

Many of the couples who contributed to this book acknowledged that praying together has become important. Many of them attend daily Mass or Adoration. Most of the deacons and their wives pray the Liturgy of the Hours together. One couple spoke of visits to shrines and the Holy Land. Another couple prays the Rosary together every morning.

But even those who prayed together also had their own prayer preferences. Several people said their private prayer experiences include meditation, special devotions, spiritual reading, and going outdoors on a prayer walk to appreciate God's creation.

### The Importance of Faith

Studies show that faith becomes more important to people as they grow older. Ninety percent of older people consider themselves spiritual or religious. About half attend religious services weekly.[59]

One woman suggests that a view toward eternal life can be a motivating spiritual factor. "I have come to realize that I am looking for something beyond this earth," she says, "and my faith is a great comfort."

Another woman says she feels a deeper sense of peace as she gets older. "There is less of a struggle," she says. "There's less searching. There is more a sense of 'I know.' The older I get, the more confidence I have in my faith."

Deacon Ken Henry also sees a firmer understanding among older adults of what it means to be Catholic. "It is a given for them that God is God, and they are not God," he says. "They recognize that life is not all about them."

## Something to Ponder

Faith does not merely gaze at Jesus, but sees things as Jesus himself sees them, with his own eyes: it is a participation in his way of seeing. In many areas in our lives, we trust others who know more than we do. We trust the architect who builds our home, the pharmacist who gives us medicine for healing, the lawyer who defends us in court.

We also need someone trustworthy and knowledgeable where God is concerned. Jesus, the Son of God, is the one who makes God known to us (cf. *Jn* 1:18). Christ's life, his way of knowing the Father and living in complete and constant relationship with him, opens up new and inviting vistas for human experience.

—Pope Francis[60]

## Questions for Reflection

1. How would you describe the stages of faith that you have experienced?

2. How has your faith changed as you have grown older?

3. How has your prayer changed?

# CHAPTER 18

# The Presence of God

When Sr. Marie Schober does workshops for older adults, she starts with this *Baltimore Catechism* question: "Where is God?"[61] "The *Catechism* tells us that God is everywhere," she says. "But somehow we get lost in the idea that God is only in certain places and in certain people and in certain things."

To illustrate her point, she tells a story about a little fish who asks an older and wiser fish to help him find the ocean. "You are *in* the ocean," the older fish replies. "No! This is only water," the little fish says as he swims away. "Are we not like the little fish?" Sr. Marie asks the workshop participants. "God is everywhere. God is in us. God is in other people. God is in all of creation. We just need to stop and pay attention. We need to take time and be quiet."

Sr. Marie teaches them a simple technique. She asks them to sit quietly and become aware of their breathing. She suggests having a prayer word like "Jesus" that they can repeat to help them refocus if they become distracted.

"As their breathing begins to slow down, I ask them to be aware of God's presence," she says. "Imagine yourself being loved and embraced by God. Rest in God's love."

The response to the sessions is always positive. "Everyone is living a fast-paced life," Sr. Marie explains. "Becoming more aware of God's presence can help people live a more loving life. They might think nothing happened in that ten minutes of silence, but if they do it every day, they will see a difference in their lives."

## God's Presence

Sr. Marie assures people that she is not trying to replace their choice of prayers or their way of praying. Instead, she wants to enhance all kinds of prayer by helping people to center their minds and hearts on the presence of God. "I try to give them ways during the day to remind themselves that God is present, such as when they get in their cars or when they take a drink of water," she explains. "Someone suggested that you can set an alarm on your phone or have a saying pop up on your computer to remind you of God's presence."

During his general audiences, Pope Francis frequently asks people to pause for silent prayer. He speaks of silence as a path to recognizing God's presence in the depths of our hearts.

"Let us never tire, therefore, of seeking the Lord—*of letting ourselves be sought by him*—of tending our relationship with Him in silence and prayerful listening," Pope Francis says. "Let us keep our gaze fixed on Him, the center of time and history; let us make room for His presence within us."[62]

St. Teresa of Calcutta recommended that the Missionary Sisters of Charity spend at least half of their prayer time in silence. "This will bring you closer to Jesus," she said.[63]

## The Present Moment

Increasing our awareness of God's presence helps us recognize that we experience God only in the present moment. If our thoughts are caught up in the past, we miss the presence of God in the now. If our thoughts focus on what is going to happen in the future, we miss God in the now. When it feels as if God is absent in our lives, it is often because our thoughts are not in the here and now.

"The present is all we have," one woman says. "The present moment is our gift. I saw a quote the other day that said, 'If you're depressed, you're living in the past. If you are anxious, you're living in the future.' We need to learn from the past and learn from our mistakes. We can dream and plan. But we also need to be mindful of what is happening right now. We need to do our best to stay in the day. We need to live mindfully."

When this woman talks about mindfulness, she is referring to breathing exercises that help you clear your mind, focus on the present moment, and accept the present moment without any stray thoughts.

Mindfulness is essentially a secularized version of the kind of silent prayer techniques that Sr. Marie Schober teaches. "People learn mindfulness techniques when they go to stress reduction workshops and to counseling sessions," she says. "The difference is that with silent prayer, we discover the presence of God in us and the presence of God in the present moment."

Another woman admits that she didn't fully understand the importance of the present moment until she retired. "I am learning to live in the moment as opposed to knowing ahead of time exactly how my day will begin and end," she says. "I love being able to just *be in the now*. I think I have finally grown into myself."

## Becoming a Better Person

Prayer brings us closer to God, and at the same time, it changes us. "When you begin to recognize God's presence, you see things from a different perspective," Sr. Marie says. "You begin to see other people as having God in them, even if you don't like them. Once you see God in other people, your attitude toward them begins to change. You may need to get over not liking their looks or their opinions or the things they do, but then you can start looking at them as a person who was created by God. When that happens, you discover something about that person, and you discover something about yourself."

Studies also show that any kind of quiet prayer is good for you physically and emotionally.[64] Dr. Herbert Benson, a cardiovascular specialist at Harvard Medical school, identified what he calls "the relaxation response" that is connected with prayer and results in a decreased heart rate, lower blood pressure, and more regular breathing patterns. It can reduce pain, stress, depression, insomnia, and some of the other challenges that can be associated with aging. The greatest benefits occur when people set aside ten to twenty minutes of quiet time once or twice a day.

Ultimately, the practice of silent prayer not only helps you to become aware of God's presence and to grow in holiness, but it also helps you to understand who you are as a child of God and what your purpose is in life.

## STRESS AND SPIRITUALITY

Stress is our body's response to danger. When we are under stress, our body releases hormones designed to help us fight or flee whatever is threatening. Adrenaline increases our heart rate, raises blood pressure, and pumps oxygen into our muscle tissue. Cortisol, another stress-related hormone, puts our brains on high alert. When the threat is over, our bodies return to normal.

Problems arise when people are under constant stress. Stress hormones remain elevated and can lead to serious illness, memory loss, and depression. Prayer is a powerful way to relieve stress. Here are some other ways spirituality can help to reduce stress:

- Talking with a spiritual director or a trusted friend can help you release stressful thoughts and find new coping mechanisms.
- Keeping a journal can help you to express your feelings and monitor the ways you are dealing with stress.
- Reading inspirational stories can open your eyes to the way others have handled difficult situations.
- Trying to see the good in others can make you less judgmental and more accepting.
- Staying connected to God can give you the assurance that you are not alone and can help you cope with the stress in your life.

## Something to Ponder

Being useless and silent in the presence of God belongs to the core of all prayer. In the beginning we often hear our own unruly noises more loudly than God's voice. This is at times very hard to tolerate. But slowly, very slowly, we discover that the silent time makes us quiet and deepens our awareness of ourselves and God. Then, very soon, we start missing these moments when we are deprived of them, and before we are fully aware of it an inner momentum has developed that draws us more and more into silence and closer to that still point where God speaks to us.

—Henri J. M. Nouwen[65]

## Questions for Reflection

1. In what ways have you experienced the presence of God?

2. How has your experience of God changed you?

3. Do you struggle to stay in the present moment? How are you working to be more attuned to the "now" in your life?

# CHAPTER 19

# What Does God Want?

When a friend invited Carolyn McLean to a weekend retreat about prison ministry, she reluctantly agreed to attend. She had retired early to help her sick mother and didn't think she had time for anything else. When the retreat leader asked everyone why they had come to the session, Carolyn replied, "I really don't know why I'm here."

Past volunteers for the ministry wrote letters to be distributed to the retreatants during the weekend. The letters described the suffering, brokenness, and pain that women in prison endure. Carolyn received a heart-wrenching letter that was written entirely in calligraphy. She had recently started taking calligraphy classes, and it seemed like an unusual coincidence. Then suddenly Carolyn started to sob. She began to feel in the depths of herself that the Lord was calling her to get involved in prison ministry. She has been part of the prison ministry team ever since.

The group plans and presents two weekend retreats each year. "We don't go into the prison to find out why the prisoners are there or to judge them," Carolyn explains. "We are there to listen and to introduce Christ's love to them."

People sometimes ask Carolyn, "Aren't you afraid?" "Are you kidding me?" she replies. "I love to go. It's a privilege. The prisoners are very open and receptive. By the end of the weekend, they are filled with the Holy Spirit. There is nothing to be afraid of. The Lord is working in the lives of these women. The retreat team members are just facilitating it."

Carolyn McLean came to a profound understanding of where God was calling her, and that sudden understanding moved her life in a new direction.

## How God Calls

Whether we realize it or not, God is always calling us. A thought pops into our head about someone, and it might be God's way of encouraging us to reach out. Someone reaching out to us might be God's way of inviting us to try something new. A dream about a difficult situation may be God's way of helping us find an answer to a problem. We may be tempted to say something negative, but something deep inside urges us to say something positive or to say nothing at all.

Sometimes God speaks to us through Scripture, music, art, nature, and the unfolding of ordinary events. Or as with Carolyn, something unexpected happens that makes us realize God is asking us to do something specific.

"A lot of people think God wants us to do what we don't want to do or what we can't do," says Sr. Marie Schober. "I try to help people understand that God made us who we are. He wants us to be the best person we can be with all of our gifts and talents and abilities. He wants us to do what gives us life and gives life to others."

One woman admitted that she didn't want to retire from her job but was told that it was time for her to leave. "That's pretty hard for someone who loves their work," she admits.

"But I also had a strong feeling that God had a plan and that I needed to pay attention. I have always thought that environmentally, we have been poisoning ourselves, and I have personally lived a chemical-free life as much as possible in today's world. So I started a small business to teach others how to live a chemical-free life. I feel like God blesses everyone I talk to. This change in lifestyle has been life-giving for me."

Another woman also had to retire earlier than she had planned. "My faith was huge in helping me to accept the reality of the situation and to see that God had other plans in mind for me," she says. "God is so full of surprises! At almost every juncture in my life, God has called me to do different things and to live in different ways. Over the years, I developed a strong sense that God is in charge and that all will be well."

## How Do I Know for Sure?

God calls each of us in ways that are personal and unique. Our understanding that this call is truly what God wants for us can come in different ways as well. Blessed Fulton J. Sheen explained that there are two ways of knowing that something is true. There is "outer" truth that we can master, such as knowing the distance of the Earth from the sun. An "inner" truth is one that masters us, such as knowing that God is merciful.[66]

The understanding that God is calling you to something will not come as an "outer" truth. You may never have absolute certainty in the same way you know that one plus one equals two. But you will attain some level of sureness about "inner" truth.

When Yolanda Sosa was asked if she wanted to contribute her thoughts and experiences to this book, she said she had to pray and make sure it was God's will. A few days later, she agreed to help. When asked how she knew it was God's will, she said thoughts about the book kept coming back to her, and she took it as a sign that this was something God wanted her to do.

"If you live your life on the basis of what God wants you to do, then you become more aware of God's will," Yolanda explains. "God doesn't talk to me in an audible voice. He doesn't say, 'I want you to do this or that.' I just have to trust God and use the common sense and wisdom that God gave me. Sometimes, it is a recurring thought that pops into my head. Sometimes, something someone says or does confirms it."

Sr. Linda LaMagna says the understanding that God is calling her to something new usually happens in a very still manner. "It's almost like I can see it in darkness first, tucked away in a corner," she explains. "Then, over time, someone invites me to embark on something new, and I feel God has already been working out the plan. Even though I have found myself fearful in saying 'yes' to some new ministry, I have always felt the Holy Spirit setting the table little by little in front of me. I feel God smiling on me, and that empowers me to look at a new adventure."

She now feels as if God is calling her to become a spiritual director so that she can help people discern how the Holy Spirit is moving in their lives. "I felt God speak to my heart through other people who said I ought to think about becoming a spiritual director," she says. "I found a three-year program, and I am going to school for three summers to train for this ministry. I love the folks who are in the program with me. I'm seventy years old, and I'm in full-time ministry, but I'm training for another ministry. I love it!"

## The Need for Discernment

Sometimes, people know with certainty where the Holy Spirit is leading. Other times, it might not be as clear. The process of figuring out what God might be asking us to do is called discernment. The word "discernment" means "to sift apart." The first step in the process is prayer.

One couple thinks they might want to do missionary work when they retire. "We've been talking about it," they say, "but we really have to sit together and pray about it. We don't know if this is something that we want or if it is something the Lord wants us to do."

Several people said they ask God every morning to guide them throughout the day. One woman feels as if God is calling her to be more compassionate. Another recognizes that God is calling her to greater trust.

Here are several other things that can help in the discernment process:

- Keeping a journal is a good way to help you recognize a pattern regarding what God might be calling you to do.

- Talking to someone you trust can provide new insights.

- Asking other people to pray for you strengthens you in ways you may not recognize.

- Trying to imagine yourself doing whatever you think God may be asking of you, and then paying attention to whether it feels energizing and life-giving, can create clarity.

"I have always had the belief that God puts you where you belong at the right time," one man says. "Or God creates enough signs that help you know what direction you should go."

## God's Desire

"God's will" is not a term Sister Marie Schober, uses when she talks with people because it might lead someone to think God only has one idea for what they should do and how they should do it.

"God's will isn't a pegboard with only one hole for us, and we have to get the exact peg in the right hole in order to please God," she explains. "I like to say, 'God's desire.' I tell people God's desire will always lead them to the betterment of themselves and others."

Sometimes, God leads you away from something you think he wants you to pursue. When Chloe Giampaolo and Arlene Zawadzki were young, they both wanted to enter the convent. Chloe wanted to be a Carmelite, and Arlene wanted to be a Maryknoll missionary in Africa. Because of circumstances beyond their control, neither one of them became nuns. They both married and had children. Chloe became a teacher, and Arlene became a nurse.

Today they can look back on everything that unfolded in their lives and understand why God led them away from religious life. But in retirement they have both become connected to religious orders as lay associates. Chloe became a secular Carmelite and strives to live the Carmelite spirituality in the world. Arlene became a Benedictine Oblate and observes the Rule of St. Benedict in her everyday life.

"The Lord works in wonderful, mysterious ways," Chloe says. "We just have to trust him."

## Something to Ponder

My Lord God, I have no idea where I am going. I do not see the road ahead of me. I cannot know for certain where it will end. Nor do I really know myself, and the fact that I think that I am following your will does not mean that I am actually doing so. But I believe that the desire to please you does in fact please you. And I hope I have that desire in all that I am doing. I hope that I will never do anything apart from that desire. And I know that if I do this you will lead me by the right road though I may know nothing about it.

—Thomas Merton[67]

## Questions for Reflection

1. When have you felt that God was calling you to undertake some new work or direction?

2. How did you discern that it was a call from God?

3. Think of one time when the Holy Spirit led you in a direction that was totally unexpected.

# CHAPTER 20

# Dealing with Change

As part of his job, Mike Reilly taught staff development workshops on dealing with change. "There are different ways that people accept change," he explains. "Some people are innovators who create change. Some people jump on change early. Most people are in the middle and work through the change. Others accept change, but at a slower pace. Some people refuse to change."

Whether we want to admit it or not, life is full of change.

- Sometimes change is easy and fun—like trying a new recipe or buying something new.

- Sometimes change is beneficial—like learning a new skill or finding a new hobby.

- Sometimes change is challenging—like losing weight or quitting smoking.

- Sometimes change is transforming—like making a new friend or letting go of a grudge.

Spending the winter in Florida was a positive change for a couple who had recently retired. "We had a great fifteen weeks," they explain. "It allowed us to focus on our relationship. We weren't able to do that as much when we were working because we were both running in different directions. We needed this time together."

## Understanding Change

Change always involves adjusting to some new reality. Sometimes we know in advance that a change is going to take place. But one woman warns that change can sneak up on you. "You get into a routine in your daily life, and all of a sudden, the routine has changed," she says.

Change moves us from the known to the unknown in ways that are not always smooth and predictable. We can find ourselves going backwards, forwards, or even sideways. In the process, we may feel somewhat disoriented.

The biggest issue, however, is not the change itself, but how we react to whatever change we are facing. We may like the change, or we may try to fight it. In the end, no matter what we say or do, we are probably not going to stop what is happening once the wheels of change are in motion.

## Preparing for Change

You can prepare for change by asking yourself some questions and seeking answers with an open mind:

- What needs to change?
- Why is change necessary?

- When will it happen?
- How will the change be implemented?
- What good things are expected?
- What new opportunities will this change bring?

Then explore your attitudes toward the change.

- What if I believed this change was good?
- How would a positive attitude affect my behavior?
- What can I do that is positive?

## The Emotional Side of Change

While small changes are often positive experiences, big changes in our lives can produce a flurry of emotions. Our initial reaction can leave us stunned and questioning.

- We don't believe it: *This can't be true!*
- We feel shock or surprise: *How could this happen?*
- We can't imagine how this will work: *It's going to be awful!*

As planning for the change begins, new feelings emerge.

- We feel worried: *How is this going to affect me?*
- We feel angry or betrayed: *I hate this!*
- We try to think of ways to stop the change: *I can't let this happen!*

When the change occurs, emotions shift again.

- We feel a sense of loss: *Things will never be the same!*
- We feel as if our faith has been shaken: *How could God allow this to happen?*
- We feel hopelessness: *I can't do this!*

After living with the change for a while, our feelings tend to soften.

- We feel resigned: *I miss the old way, but I can live with this.*
- We feel surprised: *It's better than I thought it would be.*
- We feel happy. *I'm glad I made the change!*

## Changes with Aging

"People need to think about the changes that come with aging," says one woman. "You need to think about how you can have quality of life when you can no longer do what you might want to do."

Researchers agree that the older people become, the more difficult it can be to change.[68] But studies also show that once those changes are made, older adults find it easier to accept and maintain the changes. Here are some of the changes we may have to face when growing older:

### Physical Changes

As we age, there are some physical changes that we can avoid. We can choose not to let our hair go gray, for example. If we find ourselves getting pudgy, we can work at losing weight. But there are other physical changes that we can't do anything about, and we must find ways to adapt.

The biggest change for one man is the need to take better care of himself. "In my twenties, thirties, and forties, I pushed through injuries and pain not thinking it mattered," he explains. "But now I pay the price. I need to take things slower and pay more attention when something hurts. I've learned to back off and not push. I joke that it is not the age, but it is the mileage, and I am well past due for an oil change!"

### Social Changes

One woman admits to changes in her social life. "I don't see friends from work as much as I would have liked," she says. "Financially, I'm not able to do as many things as I would like—movies and meals out—not that I don't do these things, but they are rationed out."

One of the biggest changes for one man came with the deaths of two close friends. "We had a breakfast club, and the four of us met every Saturday morning for breakfast," he says. "Now there are just two of us who meet for breakfast. We talk about the other two guys. We imagine what they would be saying if they were still here with us."

*Lifestyle Changes*

A couple who travel a lot noticed that they have given up some spontaneity and adventure for personal comfort. "Before, when we were traveling, we might say on the spur of the moment, 'Let's get a flight and go here!' We would jump all around and not always stay in the nicest places. We don't do that anymore. People's priorities and needs change as they get older."

*Dealing with Change*

When faced with the choice to resist or to accept change, it's important to remember that this isn't the only time in your life when you've had to face change. When you look back, you realize that the only real constant in life is change. Change keeps life from becoming routine. Change often helps us to embrace a new sense of purpose, not just a new way of doing things.

Prayer can help us as we deal with change. It shifts the burden of change into God's hands. It eases discomfort, calms fear, and helps us see from a different perspective. Prayer opens our minds, hearts, and souls to God. It enables us to appreciate the good things that change can bring and to be grateful for all that God continues to do for us. When we turn to God in prayer, we give him the opportunity to fill us with deep inner peace.

## Something to Ponder

God, give us the grace to accept with serenity the things that cannot be changed, courage to change the things that should be changed, and the wisdom to distinguish the one from the other.

—Reinhold Niebuhr[69]

## Questions for Reflection

1. What age-related changes are you facing?

2. How have you dealt with change in the past?

3. In what ways have you come to an acceptance of change in your life?

# CHAPTER 21

# Making the Best of It

When Mary Ryan's cardiologist said she had to start exercising, Mary bought a stationary bike. "Of all the workout devices, it seemed to suit my lifestyle," she laughs. "I could sit, lean back, listen to audiobooks, and still feel a bit virtuous." It wasn't long before Mary's initial enthusiasm waned, and "boredom reared its ugly head."

Her daughter had an idea. She suggested that Mary "go somewhere" on her stationary bike. "It took me a minute, but I finally picked up on what she meant," Mary says. "Choose a destination, figure out the mileage, and aim for that number of miles on my bike."

Mary lives near Cleveland. She has a granddaughter near Buffalo, 197 miles away. So over the next few weeks, Mary pedaled toward Buffalo on her stationary bike. "It was actually fun to watch the miles accumulate," she says. "It was late in the day when I arrived, so I left my granddaughter a note on Facebook."

Mary felt good about achieving her goal and decided to keep going. She has a grandson in Pittsburg, 210 miles south of Buffalo. She arrived there on her eightieth birthday. "My grandson and his wife were both working, so I posted on Facebook, left a virtual bone for their dog, poured myself a glass of wine, and pondered my next trip," she says.

Mary has a daughter in Indianapolis, about six hundred miles away. "I bravely started out, but soon boredom crept in again," she admitted. "What, I thought, if I took baby steps, calculating distances in smaller segments. As I targeted various towns along my route, I became interested in them."

Using Wikipedia, Mary looked up historical places, museums, and parks. She found a treasure trove of facts about America, which she posted on Facebook along with her mileage. Over the past three years, she has pedaled four thousand miles. She "visited" two daughters, and she is on her way to "visit" two sons in the state of Washington. After that, she plans to "visit" a granddaughter in San Francisco, a sister in Santa Fe, and a niece in North Carolina.

If someone gave out awards for turning lemons into lemonade, Mary Ryan would get one. But Mary's attempt to make the best of a difficult situation is not unique. Studies show that as people age, they become increasingly adept at overcoming difficulties in a positive way.

## How Good Do You Feel?

In a recent study, researchers found that even when faced with chronic health problems such as diabetes, heart disease, arthritis, and high blood pressure, most older adults report their health to be good, very good, or excellent. According to the National Institutes of Health study, "Growing Older in America," only one in five people ages fifty-five to sixty-four said they were in fair or poor health, and only 43 percent of those over eighty-five complained of poor health. People in the sixty-four to seventy-four age group were the most positive with over 80 percent saying their health was good, even if they had health issues.[70s]

A sixty-year-old cancer survivor insists that he is in good health. "It's been two years since I was diagnosed with prostate cancer, but the choices I made for treatment have worked well," he says. "It's not detectable now, which is as good as it gets!"

A seventy-year-old breast cancer survivor also thinks of herself as being healthy. "I think it's important at this point in my life to be positive about everything," she says.

## Dealing with Pain

As people get older, they often discover that pain can become part of their everyday life, but even pain doesn't necessarily dim their spirits. One woman finds positive ways to deal with asthma, arthritis, and sensitivity to direct sunshine. "Getting older means making adjustments, and we all have to make them," she says. "I get up every day, and I keep moving—even if I'm slower, I'm still moving. I might have to give up sitting in the sun, but I can enjoy being outside in the shade. When we took our grandchildren to Disney, I ordered a scooter because I didn't know whether my asthma would be good or bad. I could use it if I needed it. That's how I tend to look at things."

Her approach is realistic and pragmatic. She has learned that you can't escape pain by denying it. Even the most powerful pain medications can't always alleviate it. But quality of life depends on how you deal with your pain.

Pain can also teach us important lessons about God, ourselves, and other people. An eighty-year-old woman sees health issues as an opportunity to offer up whatever discomfort she feels as a special way of praying for a specific intention or person. "Can't sleep?" she says. "Offer it up. Pain in your back? Offer it up. The list is endless!"

A seventy-year-old man agrees: "In no particular order, I have glaucoma, macular degeneration, multiple back surgeries, and a blood disorder," he says. "Prayer and a positive attitude are often the way to get through the day. When pain comes, I pray, 'Okay, Lord, this one's for your use.'"

Here are some of the other ways people have transformed the difficulties connected with aging into something positive and life-giving:

### Vision Problems

Several years ago, one man began to experience vision impairment because of macular degeneration, an age-related deterioration of the eye that can lead to blindness. "It has made reading difficult, restricted my driving, and limited some of my involvement as a permanent deacon," he admits. "This has caused me to give up some things and adapt to others and do things in a different way. For one thing it is impossible for me, despite magnification, to read a book from start to finish. Now, my wife and I choose books that we both want to read. She reads aloud, most days after dinner. We just finished Ron Chernow's 817-page book on George Washington! Since my vision impairment, I have also become more adept in the kitchen, and I do more cooking."

*Hearing Loss*

A woman remembers when she first began to notice a change in her husband's behavior. Formerly the life of the party, he had started to become quieter and more withdrawn. She also noticed that she was constantly repeating herself. She would say something about a store, for example, and he would ask her why she was bored. She noticed that the volume on the television kept getting louder. After a family party, she asked him why he was agreeing with everything their adult kids were saying. He admitted that he was just nodding his head because he couldn't keep up with the conversation. They began to realize that he might have a hearing problem. He went for testing and ended up with hearing aids. "I never worried about the appearance of them," he says. "Those things don't bother me. It sure makes life easier." His wife agrees. "I am really happy for him," she says. "His quality of life is so much better!"

*Joint Replacements*

When one woman reached the point at which she didn't want to do anything because her knee hurt so much, she realized it was time for a joint replacement. Her motivation for getting it done was her mother. "My mother should have had a knee replacement, but she never did anything about it," she explains. "She had such bad arthritis that she ended up on a scooter her last two or three years. I said to myself, 'I'm never going to do that.'"

After the surgery, this woman was diligent about her recovery. "I saw people in rehab who only complained and never did the exercises," she recalls. "I think it is important to keep at it. The pain from the surgery eventually goes away. It gets better every day. Then one day I realized I was walking, and I didn't have pain. I could get up from a chair without using the arms to push myself up. I was better!"

*Sleep Apnea*

After going through a sleep study, one man found out he had breathing issues. "So now I'm hooked up to a CPAP machine," he says. "It was a very positive thing because I wasn't sleeping well, but surrendering to using the CPAP helped. When the doctor tells you there are some things you need to do, you probably should do them, or you will suffer more. So, my advice is to accept the things that come your way. If you need to make changes, make the changes."

## Focusing on Good Things

Several years ago, researchers discovered a positive link between the mind and the body that can have significant benefits for older people who are dealing with chronic diseases.[71] Participants with coronary heart disease, asthma, and high blood pressure were asked to focus on things in their lives that made them feel good. They were also taught positive self-affirmation techniques to use when obstacles arose that threatened to divert them from their health care plan.

For example, the researchers asked that every morning they think about little things that made them feel happy, such as babies in hats or a beautiful sunrise. Throughout the day, they encouraged them to notice other small things that made them feel happy and to stop for a moment to savor the enjoyment. When they encountered difficulties that might interfere with taking medicine or exercising, they were asked to think about a proud moment in their lives like a wedding or a graduation or the birth of a grandchild.

The results showed that people who used the positive affirmations did better than people in the control group who did not. The takeaway message is that people can have a positive impact on their health and well-being when they try to make the best out of a difficult situation.

## OFFERING IT UP

When you "offer up" whatever pain, anxiety, or discomfort you feel for some greater purpose, you enter into what is known as redemptive suffering. It works like this: you offer your own suffering to God as a prayer in the hope that your suffering will benefit someone or some situation. You unite your pain with that of Christ on the cross. God brought good from the pain of Christ on the cross, and God can bring good from your pain, transforming it into a prayer on behalf of others. Redemptive suffering helps us to see that pain is not meaningless. You begin to recognize that God is with you, no matter what is happening in your life.

## Something to Ponder

Let nothing disturb thee;
Let nothing dismay thee:
All thing pass;
God never changes.
Patience attains
All that it strives for.
He who has God
Finds he lacks nothing:
God alone suffices.

—St. Teresa of Avila[72]

## Questions for Reflection

1. What are some of the physical limitations that you face?

2. How do you make the best of those things?

3. What have you learned about God, yourself, and other people in the process of refusing to give in to the limitations in your life?

# CHAPTER 22

# Family Matters

Jerry and Nancy McCarthy consider themselves part of the "sandwich generation." Jerry is still working full time, and they are both involved in volunteer activities. But Jerry and Nancy try to spend a significant amount of time with Jerry's ninety-four-year-old mother who still lives in the house where Jerry grew up. They also have three daughters and nine grandchildren who all live out of town.

"We do a lot of traveling!" Nancy says. "We realize that careers and accomplishments are important, but not as much as relationships with family."

Dealing with family members, whether aging parents, adult children, or grandchildren, can be a mixed blessing as we get older. On one hand, we may agree wholeheartedly with a recent Pew Research study of older Americans who said having more time to spend with family is one of the best parts of growing old.[73] But we may also feel the strain involved as family relationships begin to change.

## Family Caregivers

One sixty-nine-year-old woman works part-time and is also the primary caregiver for her ninety-year-old mother who lives alone in the family homestead. "I take care of her house and do some of the yard work," she says. "My mother does the laundry, but I worry about her going up and down the stairs. Sometimes I stay overnight if she has an early doctor appointment the next day. Yesterday morning, she started to cry because she thinks she is a burden. She has had a lot of health problems in the past year. When people are sick, everything is harder."

According to the recent Transamerica Retirement Survey, almost three out of every ten older adults are or have been family caregivers. Twenty-eight percent of them were working at the same time. Nearly nine out of ten admitted that they had missed work, taken vacation days, cut back on hours, or worked an alternate schedule at some point because of their caregiving responsibilities.[74]

Care provided by family members is often the determining factor in whether an older person can remain at home. But sometimes the older person's physical or mental condition means they need to be in a nursing home, even if family caregivers are available.

One couple is struggling with both of their mothers in nursing homes. His mother is ninety-eight and has reached the point at which she remembers nothing from minute to minute. Her mother is in her mid-eighties and is in a facility in another city, which makes it more difficult for them to visit her.

## Caring for Grandchildren

At the opposite end of the caregiving spectrum are people who care for grandchildren. In a recent Pew Research survey, 72 percent of grandparents said they helped with child care occasionally. About one in five care for grandchildren on a regular basis.[75]

For many older adults, caring for grandchildren can be a joy. But most grandparents recognize the need to set boundaries. "We will babysit during the week, but the weekends are ours," one woman says. "There are times when we tell our kids that we can't babysit, and they are okay with that."

"Taking care of grandchildren is fun, but it can also be exhausting," admits another woman. "We have to make sure we are taking care of ourselves."

A third woman says she enjoys being with her grandchildren, "but it is also great fun to watch your children as they become parents themselves."

## Dealing with Adult Children

Your children will always be your children, but as they grow into adulthood, start their own careers, marry, and have children, family relationships change. Some parents and adult children transition into new roles without any problems. For others, it might be more of a struggle.

Several years ago, Dr. Kira Birditt, a research associate professor in the Life Course Development Program at the University of Michigan Institute for Social Research, looked at tensions between parents and adult children.[76] Her team of researchers asked about personality differences, past relationship difficulties, how family members maintain contact, and feelings about adult children's lifestyle issues including finances and housekeeping habits.

Personality differences and parents offering unsolicited advice created the most long-term and deep-seated tensions. Conflicts about finances and housekeeping were more easily resolved or ignored. Researchers agreed that the best strategies for dealing with conflict involved openness, a willingness to understand and accept the other's point of view, and a desire to find solutions to problems. Confrontational behaviors such as arguments and raised voices were the most destructive strategies.

"With your adult children, you need to accept that they have their lives and friends, and they are not going to be as tied to you as they once were," one woman observed. "From my point of view, it's better to accept what they are willing to give and not try to make them feel guilty for not giving you more."

## When Adult Kids Worry

As people get older, they often notice that their adult children develop heightened concerns about them. One woman and her close-knit group of friends have decided that they will no longer tell their adult children about any mistakes they might make.

"We joke that if someone falls or someone forgets to put out their garbage, we won't tell anyone!" she laughs. "One of my friends prays that she doesn't get into a fender bender because she's worried her kids will try to take away the car keys."

John Leland, a *New York Times* reporter, spent a year visiting six elderly people and realized that their lives were fuller and more positive than he had originally assumed. "Old age remains a topic on which we middle-aged people think we know it all," he wrote. "Even after my year with the elders, I still saw my mother's life through my prejudices about old age. The life she actually led was something else."[77]

## The Power of Prayer

Sometimes, prayer is the best way to deal with family matters. Donna Kaiser remembers the years when she and her husband juggled parenting responsibilities with working full-time and caring for aging parents.

"It was during those difficult 'sandwich years' that I returned to my Rosary for comfort and to Mary for her motherly wisdom," Donna says. "I said the Memorare constantly. I began to talk to God, pray fervently to God, and even try to make deals with God. I needed help with caregiving responsibilities, a son lapsing from the church, and a daughter planning a marriage and a career. Prayer got me through those very difficult years. I would often stop at an Adoration chapel near my mother's nursing home and sit in peaceful solace, gaining more strength."

# Something to Ponder

Perfect families do not exist. This must not discourage us. Quite the opposite. Love is something we learn; love is something we live; love grows as it is "forged" by the concrete situations which each particular family experiences.
—Pope Francis[78]

## Questions for Reflection

1. In what ways do you care for members of your family?

2. How would you describe your relationship with your adult children?

3. How does prayer sustain you in your family life?

# CHAPTER 23

# Family Friction

When Teri Donner's husband, Charlie, was dying from cancer, their son, their daughter, and Teri's sister were all going through a divorce. "It was very difficult because it all happened at the same time," Teri recalls. "There was nothing we could do to fix it. Poor Charlie. He was not feeling well, and we had all these things going on."

When bad things happen in good families, it's heart wrenching. And when multiple difficulties surface at the same time, as they did in the Donner family, it can feel overwhelming. Like Teri, most people want to do something to fix whatever is going on, but that's not always possible. You can be supportive. You can listen. You can pray. But you can't change what other people choose to do or not do.

Adding to the difficulty is the feeling that your family is the only family who has ever had to face these kinds of problems. On one level, you know that's not true. But on another level, the bad situation happening in your family makes you feel isolated and alone. The reality, however, is that all families face difficulties. Some problems are big and some are small, but any problem is a struggle for the family who is experiencing it.

Here are some family problems that came to light during the interviews for this book. In most of these cases, the families didn't want their names used, but they wanted their stories shared so that people in similar situations would know they are not alone.

## Addictions

"I watched my son-in-law self-destruct from drugs," one woman said. "He had a lot of self-destructive tendencies."

"My daughter's drug of choice is alcohol," another woman said. "She won't admit that she has a problem. She went for help, but it didn't work. It is so hard to deal with it."

"Our son is an alcoholic, and we have had drug problems with some of our grandchildren," a grandmother said. "I pray for them every day."

No one chooses to become an addict. Addictions often develop gradually. The cycle starts when people discover a substance or activity that deadens emotional or physical pain and makes them feel good. Over time, they come to rely on the substance or activity and move from occasional use to regular abuse, becoming addicted. In the process, the addiction can even alter their brain cells.

It's not clear why some people become addicted and others don't. In the past, people suffering from addictions were considered morally unstable or lacking in willpower. Today, addiction is recognized as a disease that appears to have a genetic component as well as environmental, physical, and emotional factors. But these factors aren't evident in every case, and in some cases, there seems to be no connection at all.

What *is* known is that one person's addiction affects the entire family. Secrets, lies, and shame destroy relationships.

Anger and resentments fester. Fear, frustration, and feelings of betrayal are common.

"Addiction is hard because there is nothing parents can do," one man explained. "The person has to decide to change."

"My son got addicted to painkillers after a car accident," one mother said. "He switched to heroin, and then he went into treatment. He was clean for eighteen months, but after a fight with his girlfriend, he bought some street heroin that was loaded with fentanyl, and he died from an overdose. Part of me died with him."

"My son crossed that line into addiction, and he couldn't come back," another man said. "He lost his friends. He lost his job. In the end, alcohol killed him." Many people have found help through spiritual direction, family counseling, or by joining support groups such as Al-Anon.[79] Others find reading books about addiction helpful.

## Sexual Orientation

Most parents admit that their first reaction is shock when a son or daughter says they have a homosexual orientation. At some point, parents must accept that this isn't something they, as parents, can change. They also need to realize that this is the same son or daughter that they have known and loved all along.

In 1997, the United States Conference of Catholics Bishops' Committee on Marriage and Family issued a statement entitled, "Always Our Children: A Pastoral Message to Parents of Homosexual Children and Suggestions for Pastoral Ministries."[80] The bishops' goal was to help parents sort through some of the difficult questions and concerns they face. They also wanted to encourage family members to continue to love one another.

When dealing with sexual orientation, families need to be honest. Loving a child doesn't mean you love everything that child does. But your child needs the assurance that you will never sever the relationship.

"I have a son who is gay," one woman admitted. "He married his partner. I have accepted it, but it was hard."

"I have a daughter who is a lesbian," another woman said. "She cut me off for quite a while, and I prayed intensely to get back in touch with her. Now we talk on a regular basis. We have to love no matter what."

"I have two transgender grandchildren," a third woman said. "They don't want to have anything to do with me. I wrote them a letter and said if I have ever said or done anything to hurt you in any way, I ask your forgiveness. That's as much as I can do. It's in the Lord's hands."

## Divorce

It can be devastating when an adult child goes through a divorce. Many parents wrestle with conflicting emotions. One day they may feel angry and the next day sad. They may worry about grandchildren. They may struggle to cope with the unraveling of family relationships and the eroding of family traditions.

It is important to keep the lines of communication open with everyone. Listen, but resist the temptation to tell your son or daughter what to do. Don't blame and don't shame anyone. There are many factors involved in the breakup of a marriage.

Even if you feel angry or resentful, don't let it show. Put the problem in God's hands. Ask God to give you the strength and the wisdom to help everyone in the family through this painful time.

"My daughter is getting divorced, and it's tearing me apart," a father admitted. "I hate to see her going through this kind of pain."

"My son and daughter-in-law were both at fault for the breakup of the marriage," another man admitted. "I worry most about my grandchildren who are angry and acting out. Sometimes the only thing you can do is pray."

## No Longer Catholic

Dealing with adult children and grandchildren who reject the Catholic faith is difficult for many older adults. One woman was so upset that she told a priest during Confession that none of her four adult children are "regular" Catholics. The priest asked if they were good people, and the woman replied that they were very good people. "The priest told me that God would take care of my children," the woman said. "That helped me. I still worry, but it's not as pressing."

This woman is not alone. According to Pew Research, 13 percent of all adults in the United States are fallen-away Catholics—people who were raised in the faith but now identify as having no religion, as being Protestant, or as having some other religion.[81]

"My kids went to Catholic school, and they both left the Church," one man said.

"None of my children go to church regularly," a woman admitted. "I spend my life now praying for them to return to the Church. I will spend my heaven doing the same thing."

"My granddaughter told her mom a couple of weeks ago that she really doesn't have any reason for God to be in her life," another woman said. "I pray for her. Miracles do happen."

## Severed Relationships

When family relationships are severed, it can be spiritually and emotionally devastating. Sometimes it happens abruptly in anger. Other times, there is gradual distancing that ends with someone leaving or being forced out of the family.

Even if one side is right and the other side is wrong, it's important to keep the lines of communication open. You don't have to agree with what a family member is doing. You can be honest and say you don't approve. But try to maintain a lifeline between that person and the family.

"There's a family in our parish that has two married daughters who don't talk to each other," one man said. "They can't have family gatherings together. Everything needs to be separate. It's awful."

"We have a son who has cut himself off from the family," another man admitted. "His wife never liked us, so we don't see our son or our grandchildren."

"It's hard," a mother says. "I try to be accepting and keep everyone together, but there's not much you can do if family members cut each other off."

## Dealing with Difficulties

Several people spoke about adult children and grandchildren who were struggling with mental illness and eating disorders. Others talked about adult children who were still living at home or were unable to find a good job with a decent salary. There were grandchildren living with boyfriends or girlfriends. There were granddaughters who had babies out of wedlock and granddaughters who had abortions. There were grandsons who were in jail.

One father said it is more difficult to watch your children go through difficulties than it is to go through them yourself. "When you are going through a family crisis, it trumps all of your other plans," he says. "Family has to come first. It's important for you to always be there. It's important to be non-judgmental. Offer to help, but don't offer unsolicited advice. Wait until they tell you what you can do to help."

Sometimes the parents who are the most successful at navigating through difficult family situations are the ones who rely on their faith. "It is hard to see family members struggle and not be able to provide much assistance," one man admitted. "I have always relied on my Catholic faith in times of struggle. I'm not afraid to ask others to pray if I need their prayers."

"Whenever we have a family crisis, I turn to God," one woman says. "He sees a bigger picture than we do. He loves my children more than I do. It's in his hands."

Sometimes, parents who find the greatest sense of peace in turmoil are the ones who focus on unconditional love. "Loving someone is sometimes a daily conscious decision," one woman explained. "But I think the biggest thing I've learned over the years is that I can still love someone even if I don't like them or if I don't like the things they may do."

"No one is perfect," another woman said. "We all make mistakes. Sometimes you just need to accept what's happening, even if it is not what you would have wanted."

## PLANTING SEEDS

In their ministry to members of the Catholic Grandparents Association, Deacon Ken Henry and his wife, Marilyn, see firsthand some of the struggles people face in families. They recognize that the world has changed and that bad things happen, but older adults are in a unique position to plant seeds of faith, hope, and love in family members, even if they never see those seeds come to fruition.

Pope Francis says the symbol of sowing seeds presents a powerful example of how God works in our lives. "A seed that sprouts is more the work of God than the man who sowed it (cf. *Mk* 4:27)," he explains. "God always precedes us. God always surprises us."[82]

## Something to Ponder

Don't let anxiety take control of your heart; each day will tell you what you are to do. You have already passed through a number of trials by the grace of God; the same grace will be there for you in all the occasions to come, and will free you from difficulties and rough paths one after the other even if God must send an angel to carry you over the more dangerous steps.

—St. Francis de Sales[83]

## Questions for Reflection

1. What are some of the family difficulties that you have had to face?

2. How did you find the wisdom and strength to deal with these problems?

3. What advice would you offer to someone who is struggling with difficult family situations?

# CHAPTER 24

# To Forgive and to Be Forgiven

Deacon John DeWolfe will never forget the day he was at Mass, and the Gospel reading included this passage: "So if you are offering your gift at the altar, and there remember that your brother has something against you, leave your gift there before the altar and go; first be reconciled to your brother, and then come and offer your gift" (Matthew 5:23-24).

The words cut to the depths of John's soul. He had divorced his first wife about ten years before. They had maintained contact over the years because of their two daughters, but John knew that the pain of the divorce still lingered for all of them. He also knew that he had to do something to reconcile with his ex-wife.

He went to her house and they talked. "I got down on one knee and asked her to forgive me," John says. "I told her that I forgive her too. We were both crying. It was such a relief. Later I went to each of my daughters and asked for their forgiveness."

But that's not the end of the story. The marriage had been annulled, and John had married again. His ex-wife had also remarried in the Catholic Church, and after the forgiveness episode, the two couples became close friends. When John was ordained a deacon in 2002, his ex-wife and her husband were there.

Several years later, John's ex-wife was diagnosed with cancer. Before she died, she asked John to serve at her funeral Mass and to assist with her burial. When her husband died, John officiated at his funeral.

"Forgiveness is a powerful thing," Deacon John says. "The incident lifted everything off our shoulders. After that it was easier for me to forgive because I had experienced the results of it. I've seen so many people hold grudges and hate against another person. It just eats people up inside."

## Choosing to Forgive

Forgiveness is a choice. We may not feel like forgiving. The other person may not want our forgiveness or deserve to be forgiven. But in choosing to forgive, we free ourselves from anger, frustration, resentment, and thoughts of revenge.

Forgiveness allows us to drain the poison out of a wound so that it can heal. It helps us to feel physically, mentally, and emotionally whole. But there is also a spiritual component to forgiveness.

"Jesus tells us that if we can't forgive, then we won't be forgiven," one woman says. "It sincerely scares me that I might not be forgiven, so I try hard to be a forgiving person. I try to love the sinner and hate the sin. I try not to judge anyone. I may think I know all about a person, but that's rarely true. I don't have to like them or like the wrong that they did. We all make mistakes, including me. Scripture tells me that if I judge someone, then I will be judged also, so I try hard to let God take care of the judging."

"Conflict is inevitable," another man says. "The best we can do is strive to be the first to forgive and the first to ask for forgiveness when appropriate. We have to realize we can't control others, but we can control our reactions to them."

## How to Forgive

Forgiveness doesn't happen automatically. It begins with your willingness to forgive. Start by telling God that you want to forgive this person, and then ask for God's help. But even after you've expressed your desire to forgive, don't be surprised if feelings of anger or resentment return.

"Every time I think I've truly forgiven, painful memories from the past resurface, and it's like the whole thing is happening all over again," one woman admitted.

Sometimes you need to keep reminding yourself that forgiving is something that you really want to do. Sometimes you just have to say out loud to yourself or to someone else, "I want to forgive! I want to let go of this pain!" It can help to write down a statement of forgiveness and then burn the paper, allowing the smoke to become a symbol of giving it to God.

Praying for the person you are trying to forgive can also help. Say an Our Father or a Hail Mary every time you think about that person as a sign to God and to yourself that you have forgiven this person. It's a good idea to keep praying for yourself too.

## Asking for Forgiveness

When you have hurt someone—intentionally or unintentionally—seeking that person's forgiveness requires prayer, reflection, and humility. Start by taking responsibility for what happened.

Don't try to excuse or rationalize it. Then think about how you would feel if someone did this to you.

Pray that God will help you to make the situation right. Pray that the other person will be gracious enough to forgive you. Then ask God to forgive you.

When you seek forgiveness, you must do it sincerely, with honesty. Even if the pain you caused was unintentional, tell the person you realize how upset and wounded they are. Then accept whatever happens next. Be grateful if the person forgives you. Be understanding if the person isn't ready to let it go. Then continue to pray for them and for yourself.

## Forgiving Yourself

Sometimes, the hardest person of all to forgive is yourself. You may struggle with guilt or regret over something that happened in the past. You may chastise yourself for immaturity, stubbornness, selfishness, or refusing to be kind. You may feel a deep sense of failure.

You can't detach yourself from what was, but if you keep thinking about what you should have done or what you regret, you're going to be paralyzed with guilt. You can be aware of what you've done but at the same time recognize that you're now living in the present moment. God loves you. God is forgiving and merciful.

The Sacrament of Reconciliation can help you to accept God's forgiveness and to forgive yourself. When you confess your sins and the priest says the words of absolution, you can begin again with a clean slate. No more shame. No more guilt.

No more fear. You allow the Holy Spirit to heal you, spiritually and emotionally. You begin to recognize God's presence in your life. You feel gratitude for all the good things in your life and for God's peace.

This kind of peace is the essence of spiritual healing. It is the peace the world cannot give. It is a gift from a loving God.

## Be Patient

"Forgiveness gets easier as people get older," Deacon John says. "It is easier to let go or to try to understand the other person's point of view instead of holding a grudge or getting angry. It is easier to accept the apology of someone who hurt you."

Sometimes, you just need to be patient.

"It took me a long time to understand forgiveness," one woman admits. "One day I just stopped trying. I'd been trying to do that forever, and it wasn't working. I found myself saying to God, 'I'm going to stop worrying about these things. If you want me to do something, let me know.' Gradually, I began to feel a sense of God's presence, a sense of faith, and I think I have a less complicated faith. I know that I am loved and I am forgiven."

## Something to Ponder

Human life needs love. And what is authentic love? It is what Christ showed us, namely, mercy. The love we cannot forego is forgiveness, which accepts those who have wronged us. None of us can survive without mercy; we all need forgiveness.

—Pope Francis[84]

## Questions for Reflection

1. When have you had to forgive someone?

2. When have you had to ask for forgiveness?

3. What is the most difficult aspect of forgiveness for you?

# CHAPTER 25

# Dealing with Loss

It never occurred to Joe McBride that his wife, Donna, would die before he did. But nine months after Donna was diagnosed with a rare form of cancer, she was gone. "We knew how important every minute was after she was diagnosed," Joe recalls. "We sat on the couch and talked about everything."

Joe and Donna had dated through high school and college. After they got married, they taught classes in English as a second language in Japan and Hawaii. Then they settled down in New Jersey and raised two children. They were planning for retirement when Donna got sick. "When Donna passed, it broke my heart," Joe admits. "I felt like the biggest piece of my life had died."

## The Pain of Grief

Grief is not an illness or a disease; it's a normal reaction to the death of someone you love. The word "bereavement" means "to be torn apart." When someone you love dies, a part of your life is torn away, and you are left with a deep emotional wound. Grieving is the process by which healing takes place.

"It wasn't the big holidays that were the hardest for me," Joe recalls. "I had enough adrenaline to carry me through those times. It was the everyday things that would get to me. It was making coffee for just me in the morning or watching

*Jeopardy* by myself. I remember driving down the road one day and starting to cry so hard that I couldn't see. I had to pull over because it wasn't safe to drive in that emotional state."

With the help of family members and friends, Joe was able to work through his grief. "A friend who lost her husband told me that there would come a time when I would laugh more than I would cry," he recalls. "She was right. You reach a point at which you can smile at memories instead of crying over them."

## No Set Path

Each person experiences grief differently, and there's no timetable for how long grief lasts. Some people try to avoid, deny, or postpone their grief, but it only makes the process more difficult. Working through grief is necessary for your emotional and physical well-being.

Most people experience physical symptoms of grief—loss of appetite, insomnia, low energy, feelings of weakness. Some people struggle with forgetfulness, anxiety, and nervousness. Sometimes, something out of the ordinary happens and brings unexpected comfort. Six months after her husband died, one woman remembers walking up the stairs in her home when she felt a touch on her shoulder. "I turned around, and nothing was there," she recalls. "But after that, I knew that my husband was watching out for me."

## Finding Ways to Cope

Teri Donner, whose husband, Charlie, died after a five-year battle with cancer, admits that there are still times when she feels lonely, confused, and sometimes angry—especially when she encounters married couples who seem to take each other for granted. "I let myself feel that way for a little bit because I think we have to allow our emotions to be real," she says. "But then I do something that I like. It might be as simple as going for a walk or calling a friend."

For the past three years, on the date of her wedding anniversary, Teri has invited a group of friends to come to her house for a girls' night. "We drink wine and toast Charlie and me at the beginning of the evening. Everyone looks forward to it, and it is better for me than sitting home alone with a picture of Charlie and a candle!"

But Teri is quick to recognize that her way of grieving might not be best for other people. "I knew Charlie was going to die," she explains. "We had time to talk before he died, and he told me that he wanted me to go on with my life and do things that make me happy. I have a friend whose husband dropped down on their bedroom floor. It was shocking. She had a completely different experience of grieving."

"You have to find your own way of getting over what happened," admits a man whose wife died from cancer. "It might take a while. Don't rush it. It will happen when it's supposed to happen."

## Living Alone

One woman always thought that if something happened to her husband, she would want to live with a family member or find a roommate. "But now I find that I'm very content to live alone," she says.

Another woman admits that it was not easy at first. "I've learned to adjust," she says. "I learned to make the best of it."

Six months after Teri Donner's husband died, her son asked her how she felt about living alone. "I miss your father every day," she replied, "but it's not horrible. I keep busy. I find things I can enjoy doing on my own, and I make my own decisions."

Her son said, "Mom, embrace that. I've had to learn to live alone for much of my life too. I had to learn to fill my time with things I like to do and make my life my own. Embrace the things that make you who you are."

## Relying on Faith

After his wife died, people asked Joe McBride if he was mad at God. "I would tell them no, I'm not angry at God because I have been given so much. The Lord has given me much more than he has taken from me."

"Faith definitely helps because you don't feel as if death is the end," Teri Donner says. "Charlie was not afraid to die. His father died when his mother was three months pregnant with Charlie, so Charlie was looking forward to meeting his father in heaven. He also had a brother who died in infancy. I believe that there is something beyond this earth. I believe God will connect us in heaven."

## The End of Bereavement

For most people, grief does not last forever. Some signs that you are ending your time of bereavement include the following:

- You begin to laugh again.

- You notice things in life that make you feel grateful.

- Eating and sleeping patterns become more normal.

- Your energy level increases.

- You establish new routines.

- You begin to look forward to events.

- You understand that your life will go on—not in the same way as before, but in a way that is satisfying and meaningful.

## Something to Ponder

This beautiful prayer helps us to place our deceased loved ones in the hands of God. It is attributed to Fr. Bede Jarrett (1881–1934), an English Dominican friar.

We seem to give them back to Thee, O God; who gavest them to us. Yet, as Thou didst not lose them in giving, so do we not lose them by their return. Not as the world giveth givest Thou, O Lover of Souls. What Thou givest, Thou takest not away, for what is Thine is ours also if we are Thine. And life is eternal and love is immortal, and death is only an horizon, and an horizon is nothing save the limit of our sight. Lift us up, strong Son of God, that we may see further; cleanse our eyes that we may see more clearly; draw us closer to Thyself that we may know ourselves to be nearer to our loved ones who are with Thee. And while Thou dost prepare a place for us, prepare us also for that happy place where Thou art we may be also for evermore.[85]

## Questions for Reflection

1. In what ways have you experienced the pain of grief?

2. What kinds of things helped you through the grieving process?

3. In what ways did your faith help you through your grief?

# CHAPTER 26

# Accepting Death as Part of Life

Mark Piscitello was at Mass one Sunday morning when he started feeling light-headed. He broke out into a sweat, his skin turned gray, and his heart started thumping. He remembers an older gentleman sitting down next to him and saying, "Everything is fine. You are all right. Everything will be okay."

But Mark wasn't okay. He passed out and his wife, Debbie, who is an intensive care nurse, couldn't find his pulse. By the time the paramedics arrived, Mark had started to regain consciousness. As they were getting ready to load him into the ambulance, Mark asked Debbie where the older gentleman had gone.

She told him there was no older gentleman. "There was!" Mark insisted. "I talked to him. He had his hand on my shoulder."

"Mark, I thought you were dead," she replied. "There was no older gentleman!"

Mark believes the older gentleman was the Lord assuring him that everything was going to be all right. Mark will tell you now that he has no fear of death.

It's not unusual for people who have had a serious accident, an illness, or a near-death experience as Mark did to come to a peaceful acceptance of their own death.

## Accepting Reality

"God gives us a finite amount of time," says a seventy-seven-year-old man. "As we age, we get more in tune with that fact." A woman recalls seeing a poster of a grandparent holding a child's hand. "There was an hourglass beside each one of them," she says. "One hourglass was full, and the other was half empty. Grandparents and grandchildren are sometimes more conscious of time."

One grandmother remembers the day her eight-year-old grandson asked if she would be alive when he graduated from high school. "I told him that I hope so," she said. "I told him most people live long lives. He seemed satisfied with that response, so I didn't go any further with it."

## Understanding Life Expectancy

The current life expectancy in the United States for a child born today is seventy-seven-and-a-half years, an average calculation that takes into consideration people who will die at a younger age as well as people who will die at an older age.

As people get older, their life expectancy actually increases because they have survived car accidents, overdoses, disease, and other forms of premature death. For example, based on calculations from the Social Security Administration, a man born in 1955 who turns sixty-five in 2020, can expect to live to eighty-two years and nine months. A woman will, on average, live to eighty-five-and-a-half years. Ten years later, when the same man turns seventy-five, he will have a life expectancy of eighty-six years two months and the woman will have a life expectancy of eighty-seven years nine months.

But remember, these numbers are only averages. No one knows the exact moment they will die. Some people don't want to think about it. Others do.

One woman admits that when she gets together with friends, they sometimes talk about death. "We talk about what it will be like to die, and how we feel about that, and how we should live our lives now," she says.

"I'm sure no one wants to die," another woman says, "but as you age, it finds its way into your thoughts. One thing I did that I feel good about is I told my niece that if I die tomorrow not to be too sad because I've had a wonderful life. I didn't tell her that just to make her feel good. It's truly how I feel. I don't know why some people have this attitude and others feel dread."

## Facing Death

When you face your own death, you accept the fact that you came into this world, that you are going to exit this world, and that you can't stop the process. You can begin to live with a freedom that you've never known before. You take every single moment and live it fully and authentically.

Acknowledging that your life will end at some point has other benefits:

- It helps you set priorities.
- It makes you want to finish things that you've left undone.

- It gives you a deeper understanding of what it means to love and to be loved.
- It strengthens your faith as you begin to see death as a transition from one state of being to another.

"As you get older, you look at the time you have left differently," an eighty-year-old woman says. "You realize that this might be the last car that you buy, and you take pleasure in the purchase of that car. Or this might be your last vacation at the beach, and you savor those moments. It's a different perspective on life."

## Getting Things in Order

One man spent the last year straightening out what he calls his temporal realities—bank accounts, beneficiaries, insurance policies, his will, and his advanced medical directives. "I've had comments from people about how this is morbid," he says. "But we are all going to die. We can make it easier for the people who are left or not. There are horror stories out there about people dying, and no one knows the family treasures are in a coffee can somewhere. I got myself prepared so that my kids don't have to worry about it."

Here are some of the important end-of-life decisions that people make:

### Advance Directives

Advance directives are your stated preferences on health care in the event that you become unable to speak for yourself. Under the advance directives umbrella, the most important element is naming a health care proxy. The proxy is the person you authorize to speak for you and carry out your wishes if you cannot speak for yourself.

Ellen Zupa worked as the director of nursing in a large cancer hospital. She understands the importance of a health care proxy. She urges people to select a family member or friend who will be available. "We just got a call from my husband's cousin who is in the hospital, but her health care proxy is in another state and could not be reached," Ellen says. "You have to think about these things before you select someone."

Ellen also urges people to make sure their wishes are clearly stated. This is often done with a document called a living will that outlines preferences regarding life support, resuscitation, feeding tubes, surgery, and pain medications, and it also lists the name, address, and telephone number of your healthcare proxy.

"The proxy should do what the person wants—not what the proxy wants," Ellen explains. "The proxy can't overrule the patient. Make sure your proxy is someone who will follow your instructions." A health care proxy only handles health care issues. "It stops at death," Ellen says, "so your health care proxy will not be able to enact wishes for your funeral or burial."

### Preplanning Arrangements

In a recent survey, 62.5 percent of respondents recognized the importance of preplanning their funeral, but only 21.4 percent had done it. The reasons they cited included "not a priority," "have not thought about it," and "too costly."[86]

The main advantage of preplanning is that it takes the burden off your loved ones, and it gives you the assurance that your wishes will be carried out. Most funeral homes today offer preplanning services. They may encourage you to prepay, but you don't have to. You can make all the decisions so that when you die, your family only has to make one phone call to the funeral home. For example,

- You can choose burial or cremation or an environmentally-friendly "green" burial that eliminates embalming and the use of metal caskets.
- You can prepurchase a cemetery plot and gravestone.
- You can specify if you want a wake and whether you would prefer an open or closed casket.
- You can preselect a casket, flowers, and prayer cards.
- You can plan your funeral Mass readings and music.
- You can specify your preference for pallbearers.

Preplanning doesn't guarantee that every one of your wishes will be carried out, but it does make clear what you want.

### Legal and Financial Decisions

If you don't have a will, now is the time to have one drawn up. If you die without a will, you have died intestate, meaning that the laws in your state will control how your property is distributed. It's possible to write your own will, but unless it's notarized and meets all your state's requirements, you may end up creating a legal nightmare for family members. It's usually worth the time and money to contact a lawyer.

It's also a good idea to have a folder with insurance policies, investments, and bank accounts with the names and telephone numbers of contact people. Don't forget to make a list of passwords so that your family can access your computer and your online accounts.

It's not easy to face your own mortality. You may find that you can deal with all of this only in small doses. But it's worth the effort. An eighty-three-year-old woman agrees. "I have lived the bulk of my life, and anytime could be the right time for me," she says. "I's not afraid to die. My first prayer in the morning is 'Thank you, Lord, I am one day closer to eternity.' My last prayer at night is 'Father, into your hands I commend my spirit' because I may not wake up the next day."

## MAKING MORAL END-OF-LIFE DECISIONS[87]

As Catholics we believe that life is sacred from birth to natural death. Euthanasia and physician-assisted suicide are always morally wrong.

The Church insists that "ordinary means" should be observed when someone is sick or dying. These ordinary means include cleanliness, food and hydration, respect, dignity, appropriate medication, and adequate pain relief.

The Church does not insist that life be prolonged without restrictions. It is morally acceptable to refuse extraordinary treatments such as surgery, chemotherapy, and experimental drugs that offer little or no hope of recovery.

As a Catholic, you will want to include several key principles in your living will such as your desire for pain relief, the distinction between treatments that are ordinary or extraordinary, and your desire for spiritual care as your life draws to a close. Many dioceses offer online prototypes for a Catholic living will with instructions on how to download and complete the forms.

## Something to Ponder

Keep your heart free and lifted up to God, for this world is not your permanent home; you are simply passing through. With heartfelt love, direct your prayers and sighs to your eternal home, so that after death your spirit may be worthy to pass happily to the Lord.

—Thomas à Kempis[88]

## Questions for Reflection

1. In what ways have you reflected on your own death?

2. What preparations have you made for your death?

3. How has the acceptance of your own death impacted your faith or your relationship with God?

# CHAPTER 27

# The Wisdom Years

Twenty-five years ago, Pat and Mary Ryan were just entering their wisdom years. They were also moving from Rochester, New York, to Chagrin Falls, Ohio. They knew that one way of meeting new people was to get involved in their new parish, but there didn't appear to be an easy way for them to break in. They asked their pastor if they could start a group called Empty Nesters for people in the fifty and older age group. He told them to wait six months, and if they still wanted to do it, they could go ahead.

The Empty Nesters group turned out to be one of the largest ministries at Holy Angels Catholic Church, and it's still going strong. Over the years, the Empty Nesters have planned a variety of activities, speakers, day trips, hikes, picnics, plays, and parties. "It is all upbeat," Mary says. "Even our opening prayer is upbeat. But we also take care of our own. We all know each other, so when someone gets sick or there is a death in the family, we can provide support. We didn't realize it at the time, but we were all helping each other to grow older with joy, fulfillment, and wisdom."

## What Is Wisdom?

Dictionary.com defines wisdom as "knowledge of what is true or right coupled with just judgment as to action; sagacity, discernment, or insight."

But wisdom is more than knowledge or good judgment; it's the ability to see the world as God sees it. And wisdom doesn't happen because we turn a certain age; it comes to us gradually as we grow in our relationship with God. As Pope Francis has said, wisdom "comes from *intimacy with God*. . . . Wisdom is what the Holy Spirit works in us so as to enable us to see things with the eyes of God."[89]

## Recognizing Life's Lessons

One of the greatest gifts we receive during the wisdom years is the chance to look back and recognize the profound lessons life has offered us. "I sometimes look back on things, and I am amazed at how they happened," one man admits. "All of those things are pieces of the puzzle that make you the person you are today."

During our wisdom years, we begin to see that all the events of our lives teach us valuable lessons about what is truly important for ourselves, for other people, and for our world. The joys of loving relationships, the sense of fulfillment, the recognition of personal growth, the deepening of faith, the times we touched the lives of others, the times others have touched our lives, the laughter, the tears, our successes, our failures, our adventures, and the ordinariness of day-to-day moments—these lessons are embedded within us. We just need to recognize them.

Gary and Kay Aitchison encourage people to embrace who they are and claim their wisdom. "With age comes perspective," Gary says. "A lot of things that are mountains when we are younger become molehills with the passage of years. A great life lesson I've learned is patience. I've also learned that every person is important, has rights, deserves equal opportunities, and should be treated with love, respect, and dignity."

Kay adds that this is a time when we can put life lessons into practice. "Be open to accepting new ideas and new experiences from the younger generation, but own and respect your beliefs and values. Become a better version of your younger self. Be loving, kind, and fun. Keep learning and growing. Be hospitable and welcoming. We have a responsibility and an important role to play as the wisdom generation."

Dianne McMahon says she feels freer now than she has at any other time of her life. "I've learned that I can't judge other people because I don't know what is going on in another person's life. Who am I to say what someone else should or should not be doing? I don't care anymore about what other people think about me. It was so much more important when I was younger. But now I feel that if someone doesn't like me, it's fine. I probably don't like that person either! I am who I am. I'm not perfect. But I feel better about myself than I did when I was young."

## Sharing Life Lessons

Amanda and John Lauer share life lessons with engaged couples in their diocese through a program called FOCCUS (Facilitating Open Couple Communication, Understanding, and Study).[90] Here are some of the things they share:

- It isn't what happens to you in your life that counts as much as how you react to what happens.

- In the words attributed to Abraham Lincoln, "Most folks are as happy as they make up their minds to be." Happiness is something you can choose to experience at any moment, regardless of the circumstances you face.

- Love is a choice you make.

- Every person has things that are great about them and things that aren't so great. Focus on the positive.

- Recognize that you are lucky and blessed. Even in difficult situations, there is always something to be thankful for if you look closely enough.

- When disagreements come up, a good question to ask yourself is this: "Is it better to be right or is it better to love?" This can diffuse an argument in an instant.

- Life is much less complicated if you speak the truth.

- When you're speaking about a person to someone else, only say things that you would say if that other person were listening in on the conversation.

- Turn frustration into fascination by understanding that there are differences in personalities.

• Try to look at things from another person's point of view.

Sr. Linda LaMagna adds a spiritual component to the life lessons she shares: "Ask God to help you love those whom you tend to shy away from," she suggests. "You will find that God loves them and can love them through you even though you don't feel capable of love. Listen more than you speak. I've learned to listen with compassion. I've learned not to fret about little things that really don't matter. I have learned to be true to myself. I've learned to be more honest and upfront. Let Jesus live his life through you. Set aside time for personal prayer. Prayer and silence help the heart grow fond of God. God holds me. The Holy Spirit lifts me up and guides me always. Nothing is impossible with God. This is my motto. I have it on my front license plate."

## Leaving a Legacy

A recent survey of older adults showed that the legacy most of them want to leave centers more on moral stature and good works than on money and possessions. More than half of the respondents want to be remembered for their beliefs and values. Some want to be remembered for charitable donations (29 percent), and others want to be remembered for their volunteer work (28 percent).[91]

As part of their legacy, Gary and Kay Aitchison plan to leave what is known as an "ethical will" for their family members. "An ethical will could be as short as a letter or as long as a book, expressing your beliefs and wishes for your family," Gary explains. "Kay and I plan to leave such a legacy for our family, expressing our morals, values, faith and beliefs, our family heritage, family stories, and genealogy. This is much more important to us than any monetary resources we may leave."

When asked what she would like to leave as a legacy, Ellen Prozeller says she hopes to leave a legacy of love. "That's what it's all about, after all," she says. "I hope what will remain is the realization that love was at the basis of my life, what I thought, what I did, and what I would like to pass on."

Ted Sosnowski says his legacy is the recognition that he always did his best and that he never gave up. "I tried to be the best husband, father, grandfather, and friend that I could be. I loved unconditionally and tried to make the world a better place. I kept my faith and tried to be a model of a good Christian. I served God, humankind, and my country."

Mary Virginia recognizes that because love is at the core of her relationships with family members and friends, she has always been someone who can be trusted and relied upon in times of sorrow or when someone wants guidance. "It may not sound exciting," she admits. "But that will most likely be my legacy—steady, trustworthy, reliable, and strong. I'm okay with that."

Colette Byrne hopes her legacy will be the way she tried to live her Catholic faith by "knowing God's unconditional love for each and every one of us and living out that love by the way I treat my family and each person I encounter as Jesus would—loving and forgiving, over and over again."

## Something to Ponder

Trust in the LORD with all your heart,
and do not rely on your own insight.
In all your ways acknowledge him,
and he will make straight your paths.
Be not wise in your own eyes;
fear the LORD, and turn away from evil.
It will be healing to your flesh
and refreshment to your bones.

—Proverbs 3:5-8

## Questions for Reflection

1. How would you define wisdom?

2. What life lessons have you learned that have helped you grow in wisdom?

3. What legacy do you want to leave behind at the end of your life?

# Notes

1. William J. Chopik, "Age Differences in Age Perceptions and Developmental Transitions," *Frontiers in Psychology*, February 2018, https://www.frontiersin.org/articles/10.3389/fpsyg.2018.00067/full.

2. "Growing Old in America: Expectations vs Reality," PEW Research, June 2009, https://www.pewsocialtrends.org/2009/06/29/growing-old-in-america-expectations-vs-reality/.

3. George E. Condon, "A 2,000 Game Winner," *Cleveland Plain Dealer*, August 14, 1979.

4. "Thinking Positively about Aging Extends Life More Than Exercise and Not Smoking," *Yale News*, July 29, 2002, https://news.yale.edu/2002/07/29/thinking-positively-about-aging-extends-life-more-exercise-and-not-smoking.

5. Douglas LaBier, PhD, "Attitude to Aging Impacts Everything about Aging," *Psychology Today*, December 13, 2016, https://www.psychologytoday.com/us/blog/the-new-resilience/201612/attitude-aging-impacts-everything-about-aging.

6. Henri J. M. Nouwen, *The Inner Voice of Love: Through Anguish to Freedom* (New York, NY: Doubleday, 1998), 70.

7. David Snowdon, PhD, *Aging with Grace* (New York, NY: Bantam Books, 2001).

8. David A. Snowdon, PhD, "Aging and Alzheimer's Disease: Lessons from the Nun Study," *The Gerontologist*, vol. 37, no. 2, 150-156, https://www.ncbi.nlm.nih.gov/pubmed/9127971.

9. Snowdon, *Aging with Grace*, 9.

10. "Lifestyle Interventions Provide Maximum Memory Benefit When Combined, May Offset Elevated Alzheimer's Risk Due to Genetics, Pollution," *Alzheimer's Association*, July 14, 2019, https://www.alz.org/aaic/releases_2019/sunLIFESTYLE-jul14.asp.

11. St. Francis de Sales, *Golden Counsels of St. Francis de Sales* (St. Louis, MO: Monastery of the Visitation, 1994), 7.

12. "The Holmes-Rahe Stress Inventory," The American Institute of Stress, https://www.stress.org/holmes-rahe-stress-inventory.

13. Jim Harter and Sangeeta Agrawal, "Many Baby Boomers Reluctant to Retire," *Gallup News*, January 20, 2014, https://news.gallup.com/poll/166952/baby-boomers-reluctant-retire.aspx.

14. Ibid.

15. Nancy K. Schlossberg, EdD, *Too Young to Be Old: Love, Learn, Work, and Play as You Age* (Washington, DC: American Psychological Association, 2017).

16. Rev. W. P. Neville, ed., *Meditations and Devotions of the Late Cardinal Newman* (London, England: Longmans, Green & Co., 1907), 299-300.

17. "What Is 'Retirement'? Three Generations Prepare for Older Age: 19th Annual Transamerica Retirement Survey of Workers," Transamerica Center for Retirement Studies, April 2019, https://transamericacenter.org/docs/default-source/retirement-survey-of-workers/tcrs2019_sr_what_is_retirement_by_generation.pdf.

18. St. Francis de Sales, *Golden Counsels of St. Francis de Sales*, 26.

19. "What Is 'Retirement'?"

20. C. S. Lewis, *Mere Christianity* (London, England: Geoffrey Bless, 1952), 98.

21. "2018 Profile of Older Americans," The Administration for Community Living, April 2018, https://acl.gov/sites/default/files/Aging%20and%20Disability%20in%20America/2018OlderAmericansProfile.pdf.

22. "Yesterday, Today and Tomorrow," NIH Research Timelines, June 30, 2018, https://report.nih.gov/nihfactsheets/viewfactsheet.aspx?csid=37

23. Kenneth M. Langa, MD, PhD; Eric B. Larson, MD, MPH; Eileen M. Crimmins, PhD; et al., "A Comparison of the Prevalence of Dementia in the United States in 2000 and 2012," *JAMA Internal Medicine*, January 2017, https://jamanetwork.com/journals/jamainternalmedicine/fullarticle/2587084

24. Louis J. Puhl, SJ, trans., *The Spiritual Exercises of St. Ignatius of Loyola*, http://spex.ignatianspirituality.com/SpiritualExercises/Puhl.

25. Rebecca Webber, "Reinvent Yourself," *Psychology Today*, May 6, 2014, https://www.psychologytoday.com/us/articles/201405/reinvent-yourself.

26. Rev. W. P. Neville, ed., *Meditations and Devotions of the Late Cardinal Newman*, 299.

27. Eric S. Kim, PhD; Ichiro Kawachi, MD, PhD; Ying Chen, ScD; et al., "Association between Purpose in Life and Objective Measures of Physical Function in Older Adults," *JAMA Psychiatry*, October 2017, https://jamanetwork.com/journals/jamapsychiatry/fullarticle/2648692

28. *Baltimore Catechism, No. 1*, question 6, https://www.sacred-texts.com/chr/balt/balt1.htm

29. The Catholic Grandparents Association is a global organization of the faithful with branch chapters in parishes. The parish groups serve as prayer and support groups for grandparents. For information on chapters in your area or how to start a chapter in your parish, visit www.catholicgrandparentsassociation.org or call 888-510-5006.

30. Rev. W.P . Neville, ed., *Meditations and Devotions of the Late Cardinal Newman*, 301.

31. Vicki Contie, "Gene Linked to Optimism and Self-Esteem," *National Institutes of Health*, September 2011, https://www.nih.gov/news-events/nih-research-matters/gene-linked-optimism-self-esteem.

32. "Optimism and Pessimism Are Separate Systems Influenced by Different Genes," *The British Psychological Society Research Digest*, April 2015, https://digest.bps.org.uk/2015/04/21/optimism-and-pessimism-are-separate-systems-influenced-by-different-genes/.

33. Sonja Lyubomirsky, *The Myths of Happiness* (London, England: The Penguin Press, 2013), 26.

34. John Leland, *Happiness Is a Choice You Make: Lessons from a Year among the Oldest Old* (New York, NY: Sarah Crichton Books, 2018), 231.

35. Henri J. M. Nouwen, *Bread for the Journey: A Daybook of Wisdom and Faith* (New York, NY: HarperCollins, 1997), 13.

36. Federal Bureau of Investigation, "Scams and Safety, Fraud against Seniors," https://www.fbi.gov/scams-and-safety/common-fraud-schemes/seniors

37. "Older but Bolder: Older Adults Make Riskier Decisions," Max Planck Institute for Human Development, March 11, 2017, https://www.mpg.de/11155381/older-adults-riskier-choices.

38. "New Hippocampal Neurons Continue to Form in Older Adults," *National Institute on Aging*, August 15, 2019, https://www.nia.nih.gov/news/new-hippocampal-neurons-continue-form-older-adults-including-those-mci-alzheimers.

39. The Pontifical North American College in Rome coordinates the celebration of Masses in the Station Churches. Mass begins each day at 7:00 a.m. in one of the churches. Sunday Masses and the Paschal Triduum are not celebrated in the Station Churches. Additional information on the history of this tradition, a schedule of churches, and descriptions of each church can be found on the website for the Pontifical North American College, https://www.pnac.org/station-churches/the-roman-station-liturgy/.

40. Additional information on the history of the Camino, descriptions of different routes, and information on how to prepare for a Camino pilgrimage can be found at http://santiago-compostela.net/.

41. Additional information on the history of Sending Out Servants, their mission trips, and other opportunities to support their powerful ministry to the people of Guatemala can be found at http://www.sendingoutservants.org/.

42. Henri J. M. Nouwen, *Here and Now: Living in the Spirit* (New York, NY: The Crossroad Publishing Company, 1994) 16.

43. "The Healthy Eating Plate," Harvard T. H. Chan School of Public Health, https://www.hsph.harvard.edu/nutritionsource/healthy-eating-plate/.

44. Katherine D. McManus, MS, RD, LDN, "Healthy Eating for Older Adults," *Harvard Health*, June 20, 2019, https://www.health.harvard.edu/blog/healthy-eating-for-older-adults-2019062016868.

45. "Physical Inactivity: A Global Public Health Problem," World Health Organization, https://www.who.int/dietphysicalactivity/factsheet_inactivity/en/.

46. "World Health Organization Fact Sheet," https://www.who.int/dietphysicalactivity/factsheet_olderadults/en/.

47. Hallie Levine, "Is It OK to Skip Your Annual Physical?," *AARP*, October 25, 2018, https://www.aarp.org/health/healthy-living/info-2018/annual-physical-possibly-unnecessary.html

48. "Are Friends Better for Us Than Family?" *MSU Today*, June 6, 2017, https://msutoday.msu.edu/news/2017/are-friends-better-for-us-than-family/

49. "Late-Life Social Activity and Cognitive Decline in Old Age," *Journal of the Neuropsychological Society*, November 2011, https://www.ncbi.nlm.nih.gov/pmc/articles/PMC3206295/.

50. Henri J. M. Nouwen, *Here and Now*, 131.

51. Denise C. Park and Jennifer Lodi-Smith, "The Impact of Sustained Engagement on Cognitive Function in Older Adults: The Synapse Project," https://www.ncbi.nlm.nih.gov/pmc/articles/PMC4154531/.

52. Road Scholar is a nonprofit educational travel organization with a focus on older adults. Additional information on the history of the group and current travel opportunities can be found at https://www.roadscholar.org/.

53. Address of Pope Francis to Students and Teachers from Schools across Italy, May 10, 2014, http://w2.vatican.va/content/francesco/en/speeches/2014/may/documents/papa-francesco_20140510_mondo-della-scuola.html.

54. Mother Teresa, *Thirsting for God: Daily Meditations,* ed. Angelo D. Scolozzi (Ann Arbor, MI: Servant, 2000), 13.

55. Pope Francis, On the Call to Holiness in Today's World, endnote 101, http://w2.vatican.va/content/francesco/en/apost_exhortations/documents/papa-francesco_esortazione-ap_20180319_gaudete-et-exsultate.html.

56. "Evidence Mounting That Older Adults Who Volunteer Are Happier, Healthier," *Science Daily*, August 29, 2014, https://www.sciencedaily.com/releases/2014/08/140829135448.htm.

57. The Peace Prayer of St. Francis cannot be found in the writings of St. Francis, but it embraces the spirit of poverty, simplicity, and love that were hallmarks of this great saint. The prayer first appeared during World War I on a prayer card with a picture of St. Francis. *The Scholasticum: A Scholastic Institute for the Study of Scholastic Theology and Philosophy*, The Franciscan Archive, https://franciscan-archive.org/patriarcha/peace.html.

58. Pope Francis, Morning Homily, June 7, 2018, https://zenit.org/articles/popes-morning-homily-cherish-those-who-first-gave-us-our-faith/.

59. Daniel B. Kaplan, PhD, LICSW, and Barbara J. Berkman, DSW, PhD, "Religion and Spirituality in Older Adults," *Merck Manual*, May 2019, https://www.merckmanuals.com/professional/geriatrics/social-issues-in-older-adults/religion-and-spirituality-in-older-adults

60. Pope Francis, *Lumen Fidei* [The Light of Faith], June 29, 2013, 18, http://w2.vatican.va/content/francesco/en/encyclicals/documents/papa-francesco_20130629_enciclica-lumen-fidei.html.

61. *Baltimore Catechism, No. 1*, question 15, https://www.sacred-texts.com/chr/balt/balt1.htm.

62. Pope Francis, Address to the 66th General Assembly of the Italian Episcopal Conference, May 19, 2014, http://w2.vatican.va/content/francesco/en/speeches/2014/may/documents/papa-francesco_20140519_conferenza-episcopale-italiana.html.

63. Mother Teresa, *Thirsting for God*, 46.

64. Sara Martin, "The Power of the Relaxation Response," *Monitor on Psychology*, vol. 39, no. 9, 2008, 32, https://www.apa.org/monitor/2008/10/relaxation.

65. Henri J. M. Nouwen, *Reaching Out* (New York, NY: Doubleday, 1975), 136.

66. Fulton J. Sheen, *Those Mysterious Priests* (New York, NY: Alba House, 2005), 9.

67. Thomas Merton, *Thoughts in Solitude* (New York, NY: Farrar, Straus & Giroux, 1999), 79.

68. National Research Council, *When I'm 64: A Story of Love and Resilience*, (Washington, DC: National Academies Press, 2006), https://www.ncbi.nlm.nih.gov/books/NBK83771/.

69. Reinhold Niebuhr, *The Essential Reinhold Niebuhr: Selected Essays and Addresses*, ed. Robert McAfee Brown (New Haven, CT: Yale University Press, 1986), 251.

70. "Growing old in America: The Health and Retirement Study," National Institute of Health, June 2017, https://www.nia.nih.gov/sites/default/files/2017-06/health_and_retirement_study_0.pdf.

71. John Allegrante, "Positive Attitude Can Benefit Patients with Chronic Disease," https://www.tc.columbia.edu/articles/2012/january/positive-attitude-can-benefit-patients-with-chronic-disease/

72. The Order of Carmelites: https://ocarm.org/en/content/ocarm/teresa-avila-quotes.

73. Jens Manuel Krogstad, "5 Facts about American Grandparents," Pew Research, September 13, 2015, https://www.pewresearch.org/fact-tank/2015/09/13/5-facts-about-american-grandparents/.

74. "What Is 'Retirement'?"

75. "5 Facts about American Grandparents."

76. Kira Birditt, Laura Miller, Karen Fingerman, and Eva Lefkowitz, "Tensions in the Parent and Adult Child Relationship: Links to Solidarity and Ambivalence," *Psychology and Aging*, vol. 24, no. 2, 2009, 287-295, https://www.ncbi.nlm.nih.gov/pmc/articles/PMC2690709/?ref=driverlayer.com.

77. John Leland, *Happiness Is a Choice You Make: Lessons from a Year among the Oldest Old* (New York, NY: Straus & Giroux, 2018), 228.

78. Pope Francis, Prayer Vigil for the Festival of Families, September 26, 2015, https://w2.vatican.va/content/francesco/en/speeches/2015/september/documents/papa-francesco_20150926_usa-festa-famiglie.html.

79. Additional information about support available to families and about the location of an Al-Anon group near you can be found at https://al-anon.org/.

80. The complete text of "Always Our Children" can be found at http://www.usccb.org/issues-and-action/human-life-and-dignity/homosexuality/always-our-children.cfm.

81. "7 Facts about American Catholics," Pew Research, October 10, 2018, https://www.pewresearch.org/fact-tank/2018/10/10/7-facts-about-american-catholics/.

82. Pope Francis, General Audience, June 3, 2019. http://press.vatican.va/content/salastampa/en/bollettino/pubblico/2019/03/06/190306a.html.

83. St. Francis de Sales, *Golden Counsels of St. Francis de Sales*, 22.

84. Pope Francis, General Audience, October 17, 2018, http://w2.vatican.va/content/francesco/en/audiences/2018/documents/papa-francesco_20181017_udienza-generale.html

85. "We Seem to Give Them Back to Thee, O God," The Priestly Fraternity of Saint Dominic, https://www.opfraternity.org/vprayer.

86. "NFDA Consumer Survey: Funeral Planning Not a Priority for Americans," National Funeral Directors Association, June 22, 2017, http://www.nfda.org/news/media-center/nfda-news-releases/id/2419/nfda-consumer-survey-funeral-planning-not-a-priority-for-americans.

87. Detailed information on what Catholics believe about end-of-life decisions can be found on the National Catholic Bioethics Center website at https://www.ncbcenter.org/publications/end-life-guide/

88. Thomas à Kempis, *The Imitation of Christ*, trans. William C. Creasy (Notre Dame, IN: Ave Marie Press, 1989), 57.

89. Pope Francis, General Audience, April 9, 2014, 2, 1, http://w2.vatican.va/content/francesco/en/audiences/2014/documents/papa-francesco_20140409_udienza-generale.html.

90. FOCCUS Inc. USA started in the Archdiocese of Omaha on the principle that communication and problem solving are essential in a successful marriage. Trained couples offer marriage formation, enrichment, and support. FOCCUS materials include a pre-marriage inventory, a marriage enrichment inventory, and other resources: https://www.foccusinc.com/about-us.aspx.

91. Patrick J. Kiger, "Older Americans Want to Be Remembered for their Values," *AARP*, October 30, 2018.